LAW, CRIME AND LAW ENFORCEMENT

SEX OFFENDER REGISTRATION WITHIN INDIAN TRIBES

IMPLEMENTATION AND CHALLENGES

LAW, CRIME AND LAW ENFORCEMENT

Additional books in this series can be found on Nova's website
under the Series tab.

Additional e-books in this series can be found on Nova's website
under the e-book tab.

LAW, CRIME AND LAW ENFORCEMENT

SEX OFFENDER REGISTRATION WITHIN INDIAN TRIBES

IMPLEMENTATION AND CHALLENGES

ANGELICA K. BISHOP
EDITOR

NOVINKA

New York

NOTICE TO THE READER

Library of Congress Cataloging-in-Publication Data

ISBN: 978-1-63482-400-2

Published by Nova Science Publishers, Inc. † New York

CONTENTS

whenever they move, or change their employment or educational status. Section 2250 applies only under one of several jurisdictional circumstances: the individual was previously convicted of a qualifying federal sex offense; the individual travels in interstate or foreign commerce; or the individual enters, leaves, or resides in Indian country.

Individuals charged with a violation of §2250 may be subject to preventive detention or to a series of pre-trial release conditions. If convicted, they face imprisonment for not more than 10 years and/or a fine of not more than $250,000 as well as the prospect of a post-imprisonment term of supervised release of not less than 5 years. An offender guilty of a §2250 offense, who also commits a federal crime of violence, is subject to an additional penalty of imprisonment for up to 30 years and not less than 5 years for the violent crime.

The Attorney General has exercised his statutory authority to make SORNA applicable to qualifying convictions occurring prior to its enactment. The Supreme Court rejected the suggestion of the United States Court of Appeals for the Fifth Circuit that Congress lacks the constitutional authority to make §2250 applicable, on the basis of a prior federal offense and intrastate noncompliance, to individuals who had served their sentence and been released from federal supervision prior to SORNA's enactment, *United States v. Kebodeaux*, 134 S.Ct. 2496 (2013).

The Fifth Circuit's *Kebodeaux* opinion aside, the lower federal appellate courts have almost uniformly rejected challenges to §2250's constitutional validity. Those challenges have included arguments under the Constitution's Ex Post Facto, Due Process, Cruel and Unusual Punishment, Commerce, Necessary and Proper, and Spending Clauses.

In: Sex Offender Registration within Indian Tribes ISBN: 978-1-63482-400-2
Editor: Angelica K. Bishop

Chapter 1

SEX OFFENDER REGISTRATION AND NOTIFICATION ACT: ADDITIONAL OUTREACH AND NOTIFICATION OF TRIBES ABOUT OFFENDERS WHO ARE RELEASED FROM PRISON NEEDED*

United States Government Accountability Office

WHY GAO DID THIS STUDY

According to DOJ, tribal nations are disproportionately affected by violent crimes and sex offenses in particular. In 2006, Congress passed SORNA, which introduced new sex offender registration and notification standards for states, territories, and eligible tribes. The act made special provisions for eligible tribes to elect either to act as registration jurisdictions or to delegate SORNA functions to the states in which they are located. GAO was asked to assess the status of tribes' efforts to implement SORNA and the challenges they face doing so.

This report addresses, among other things, (1) the extent to which eligible tribes have retained their authority to implement, and for those that did, describe their implementation status and (2) implementation challenges tribes

* This is an edited, reformatted and augmented version of the United States Government Accountability Office publication, GAO-15-23, dated November 2014.

that retained their authority reported, and steps federal agencies have taken or could take to address these challenges. GAO reviewed data on eligible tribes' implementation status; conducted a survey of tribes that retained their authority; and interviewed federal, state, and local officials.

WHAT GAO RECOMMENDS

GAO recommends that, among other things, the SMART Office encourage states to notify tribes about offenders who plan to live, work, or attend school on tribal land upon release from prison. GAO also recommends that BIA reach out to all tribes that retained their authority to determine what, if any, assistance they would like from BIA. DOJ and Interior concurred.

WHAT GAO FOUND

Most eligible tribes have retained their Sex Offender Registration and Notification Act (SORNA) implementation authority and have either substantially implemented the act or are in the process of doing so. As of August 2014, 77 percent (164 of the 214) of eligible tribes had retained their implementation authority. Tribes that lacked the resources, among other factors, to implement SORNA either delegated their own authority, or the SMART Office delegated the tribe's authority, to a state. According to the Office of Sex Offender Sentencing, Monitoring, Apprehending, Registering, and Tracking (SMART Office)—the office SORNA established within the Department of Justice (DOJ) to administer and assist jurisdictions with implementing the law—43 percent (71 of 164) of tribes that retained their authority to implement SORNA have substantially implemented the act; the SMART Office has not yet made a final determination on 43 percent (70 of 164); and 13 percent (22 of 164) have not submitted complete packages. The SMART Office determined that 1 tribe has not yet substantially implemented SORNA.

In GAO's survey of tribes that retained their authority, the four most frequently reported implementation challenges included inability to submit convicted sex offender information to federal databases, lack of notification from state prisons upon the release of sex offenders, lack of staff, and inability to cover the costs of SORNA implementation. Federal agencies have taken steps to address these challenges, but more could be done. For example, DOJ and the Bureau of Indian Affairs (BIA) within the Department of the Interior (Interior) have formed a working group to better coordinate federal efforts to address tribes' difficulties submitting convicted sex offender information to federal databases. However, some states have not notified tribes—those that retained their SORNA authority, as well as ineligible and delegated tribes—when sex offenders who will be or have been released from state prison register with the state and indicate that they intend to live, work or attend school on tribal land, as SORNA requires; and while the SMART Office has taken some actions, more could be done to encourage states to provide notification to tribes. Such notification would help tribes identify and monitor sex offenders who live on their lands and enforce tribal laws pertaining to sex offenders. The SMART Office, U.S. Marshals Service, and BIA provided financial assistance, equipment, and staff to help tribes address their resource needs. However, BIA offered assistance only to tribes for which BIA provides direct law enforcement services, which account for only 20 percent of the tribes that retained their SORNA implementation authority, even though BIA is responsible for assisting and advising all federally recognized tribes regarding their law enforcement and public safety needs. Taking steps to ascertain what, if any, resource or other needs all tribes that retained their authority may have could better position BIA to support the tribes' efforts to implement the act.

ABBREVIATIONS

AWA	Adam Walsh Act Implementation Grant Program
BIA	Bureau of Indian Affairs
BOP	Bureau of Prisons
CJIS	Criminal Justice Information Services Division
CODIS	Combined DNA Index System
COPS	Community Oriented Policing Services
CSA	CJIS Systems Agency
DOJ	Department of Justice
FBI	Federal Bureau of Investigation
IAFIS	Integrated Automated Fingerprint Identification System
JAG	Justice Assistance Grant
JMD	Justice Management Division
JUST	Justice Telecommunications System

MOA	memorandum of agreement
NCIC	National Crime Information Center
NSOR	National Sex Offender Registry
OJP	Office of Justice Programs
OJS	Office of Justice Services
ORI	Originating Agency Identifier
OTJ	Office of Tribal Justice
PROTECT	Prosecutorial Remedies and Other Tools to End the Exploitation of Children Today
SMART Office	Office of Sex Offender Sentencing, Monitoring, Apprehending, Registering, and Tracking
SORNA	Sex Offender Registration and Notification Act
TTSORS	Tribe and Territory Sex Offender Registry System
USMS	U.S. Marshals Service

* * *

November 18, 2014

The Honorable F. James Sensenbrenner
Chairman
The Honorable Robert C. Scott
Ranking Member
Subcommittee on Crime, Terrorism, Homeland Security, and Investigations
Committee on the Judiciary
House of Representatives

In 2009, the United States Attorney General launched a Department of Justice (DOJ) initiative on public safety in tribal communities and identified combating violence against women and children in tribal communities as one of the department's priority goals. According to DOJ, tribal nations are disproportionately affected by violent crime, particularly violent crime against women. Starting in 1994, Congress passed several laws that required states to establish sex offender registries—which are systems that enable law enforcement officials to monitor convicted sex offenders who live in the state, and to establish notification systems to alert the public about these offenders.[1] Since these sex offender registration and notification laws applied only to states and territories, there were public safety concerns that convicted sex offenders would move to tribal lands to avoid registration. To protect the public, including tribal nations, from sex offenders, in 2006, Congress passed the Sex Offender Registration and Notification Act (SORNA) as Title I of the Adam Walsh Child Protection and Safety Act (Adam Walsh Act).[2] SORNA sought to introduce comprehensive standards to make state and territory sex offender registration systems more uniform. It also provided certain tribes the opportunity to create sex offender registration and notification systems where, for most tribes, these systems did not previously exist. The initial statutory deadline for implementing SORNA was July 2009—3 years after the Adam Walsh Act was enacted. However, given that none of the jurisdictions had substantially implemented SORNA by the original deadline, the Attorney General exercised his authority under SORNA to authorize two 1-year extensions of the deadline to July 2011.[3]

SORNA establishes that federally recognized tribes, with the exception of those tribes that are subject to the criminal jurisdiction of a state, under a specific federal statute, are eligible to implement the act.[4] SORNA grants authority to the states where ineligible tribes are located to implement the act on behalf of these tribes. In 2013, we reported that 19 of 56 states and territories had substantially implemented SORNA.[5] We noted that a majority of nonimplemented jurisdictions reported that generating the political will to incorporate the necessary changes to their state laws and related policies or reconciling legal conflicts between SORNA and state laws were among the greatest challenges to implementation. Since our 2013 report, the Office of Sex Offender Sentencing, Monitoring, Apprehension, Registering, and Tracking (SMART Office)—the office responsible for administering the standards for SORNA implementation— has determined that 1 additional state has substantially implemented SORNA.

Recognizing that tribes may vary in their capacities for discharging the sex offender registration and notification functions, SORNA made special provisions for eligible tribes to elect either to act as registration jurisdictions or to delegate their registration and notification functions to the states.[6] SORNA requires delegation for tribes subject to state criminal jurisdiction pursuant to 18 U.S.C. § 1162, tribes that do not elect to implement SORNA, and tribes that the Attorney General determines have not substantially implemented the act and are not likely to become capable of doing so within a reasonable amount of time.[7]

Considering the unique circumstances tribes face with eligibility and capability to implement the act, you asked us to assess the status of tribes' efforts to implement SORNA and the challenges they face with implementation. Specifically, this report addresses the following questions:

- To what extent have eligible tribes retained their authority to implement SORNA, and for those that did, what is their implementation status?
- What implementation challenges, if any, have tribes that retained their authority to implement SORNA reported, and what steps have federal agencies and others taken or could they take to address these challenges?
- To what extent are states incorporating ineligible and delegated tribes into their state sex offender registration and notification systems?

To address our first objective, we reviewed the SMART Office's data of eligible tribes' implementation status as of August 2014 to identify (1) tribes that have retained their authority to implement SORNA, (2) tribes that have delegated their implementation authority to a state, and (3) tribes whose implementation authority the SMART Office delegated to a state. To address the reliability of the SMART Office's data on tribes' implementation status, among other steps, we obtained written responses to our questions on how SMART Office representatives who use and maintain the data ensure the data's reliability. We found the data sufficiently reliable for the purpose of identifying tribes' SORNA implementation status. In addition, we surveyed the SORNA points of contact for each of the tribes that retained their authority to implement SORNA to obtain more detailed information on these tribes' implementation status. We received responses from 80 percent (129 of 161) of all tribes surveyed.[8]

To address our second objective, we interviewed legal advisers and management officials from the SMART Office, the Office of Tribal Justice (OTJ), the U.S. Marshals Service (USMS), and the Federal Bureau of Investigation (FBI), as well as the Bureau of Indian Affairs (BIA) within the Department of the Interior, to determine the implementation challenges tribes have reported and steps the agencies, the tribes, and others have taken to address these challenges.[9] In addition, we interviewed FBI Criminal Justice Information Services Division (CJIS) management and program officials to determine CJIS policies and procedures for granting tribes access to federal criminal justice databases, which CJIS manages and are required for SORNA implementation. We also interviewed state and tribal, as well as local, law enforcement officials from 5 states— Florida, Michigan, Nevada, New York, and Oklahoma. We selected these 5 states because each contains territory of tribes that retained their authority to implement SORNA, and the states vary with regard to their SORNA implementation status and geographic diversity. In addition, we interviewed management and law enforcement officials from the two BIA Office of Justice Services (OJS) regional districts that are responsible for most of the direct service tribes that retained their authority to implement SORNA.[10] We discussed with these officials what, if any, assistance they have provided to tribes with regard to SORNA implementation. Although the perspectives we obtained from our interviews with these state, BIA, and tribal officials are not generalizable, the interviews provided insights regarding the challenges that tribes face with implementing SORNA and actions that federal agencies have taken or could take to address the challenges.

We also included questions in our survey of tribes that retained their authority to implement SORNA about the types and extent of challenges the tribes experienced with SORNA implementation; steps the tribes are taking to address the challenges; and the funding and other assistance the tribes have received or could receive from federal, state, or local law enforcement agencies to assist them with implementing the act. To determine if any additional actions could address such challenges, we compared our survey results against SORNA provisions as well as the National Guidelines for Sex Offender Registration and Notification (National Guidelines).[11]

To address our third objective, we interviewed state SORNA and sex offender registry officials from all 6 states where ineligible tribes are located as well as 8 ineligible tribes—at least 1 each from the 6 states. We selected the tribes based on whether they submitted a resolution to implement SORNA in spite of their ineligibility, and the challenges the states in which the tribes are located reportedly faced with SORNA implementation.[12] The information from these interviews enabled us to determine if these states include the ineligible tribes in their state SORNA registration and notification systems, as SORNA requires, as well as to identify the challenges, if any, the states and tribes face with having the states implement SORNA on the tribes' behalf. We also interviewed tribal leaders from 4 delegated tribes that opted out or were delegated by the SMART Office, and solicited perspectives of sex offender registry officials in the 15 states to which tribes' SORNA authority has been delegated.

To supplement the information we received from our interviews as well as our survey of tribes that retained their authority, we interviewed officials from three relevant national associations: the National Congress of American

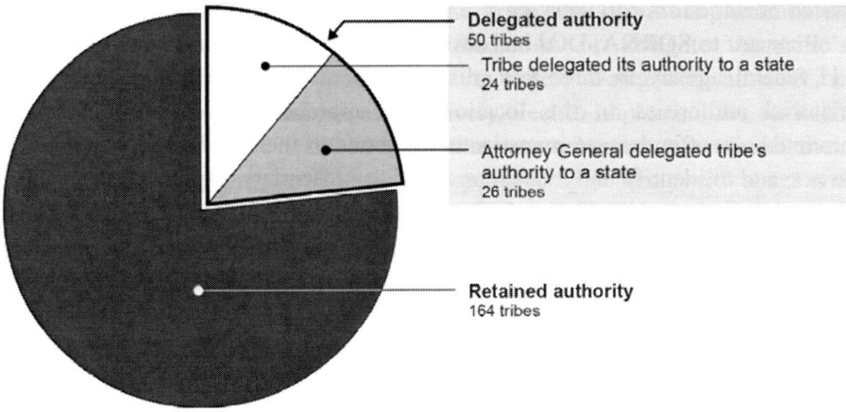

Source: GAO analysis of Office of Sex Offender Sentencing, Montoring, Apprenhending, Registering, and Tracking data. | GAO-15-23.

Figure 1. Eligible Tribes That Have Retained and Delegated Their Authority to Implement the Sex Offender Registration and Notification Act (SORNA), as of August 2014.

According to SMART Office representatives, the agency delegated the SORNA implementation authority of 26 tribes primarily because the tribes (1) chose not to delegate their authority although they did not plan to implement the act, because they thought delegating their authority was equivalent to relinquishing their sovereignty; (2) indicated that they lacked the necessary resources to implement the act in a reasonable amount of time; or (3) were nonresponsive to the SMART Office's repeated inquiries to gauge the tribes' interest in implementing the act. Our interviews with tribal council and law enforcement officials from 2 of the 24 tribes that elected to delegate their authority to a state similarly revealed that these tribes chose to delegate their authority because they did not have the necessary resources to implement the act.[26] Furthermore, officials from 1 tribe stated that implementation did not seem worth the expense for their tribe considering the small number of tribal members, the fact that none of the tribal members live on tribal land year-round, and the remote location of their tribal land.[27]

SMART Office Determined That 43 Percent of Tribes That Retained Their Authority Have Substantially Implemented SORNA, and Nearly 43 Percent More Are in Process

According to the SMART Office, 43 percent (71 of 164) of tribes that retained their authority to implement SORNA have substantially implemented the act; nearly 43 percent (70 of 164) have submitted an implementation package, but the SMART Office has not yet made a determination; and 13 percent (22 of 164) have not submitted a complete package. The SMART Office has determined, to date, that 1 tribe has not substantially implemented SORNA, as shown in figure 2 and appendix III. For the implementation status and location of all eligible tribes, see figure 3.

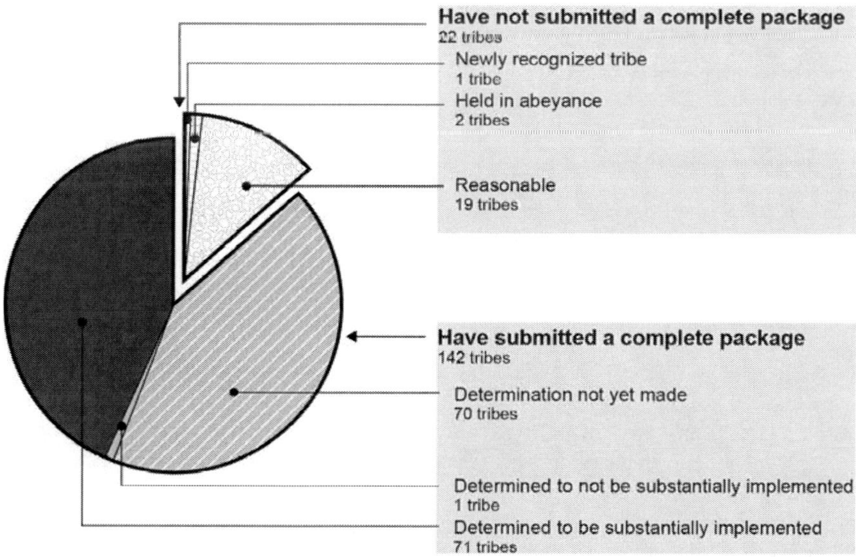

Source: GAO analysis of Office of Sex Offender Sentencing, Montoring, Apprenhending, Registering, and Tracking data. | GAO-15-23.

Note: Of the 22 tribes that have not yet submitted a complete package, 2 tribes are being "held in abeyance" because they are in the process of acquiring land. The SMART Office has granted an implementation deadline extension to 19 other tribes that it determined can implement the act in a "reasonable" amount of time.

Figure 2. Implementation Status of Tribes That Have Retained Their Authority to Implement the Sex Offender Registration and Notification Act (SORNA).

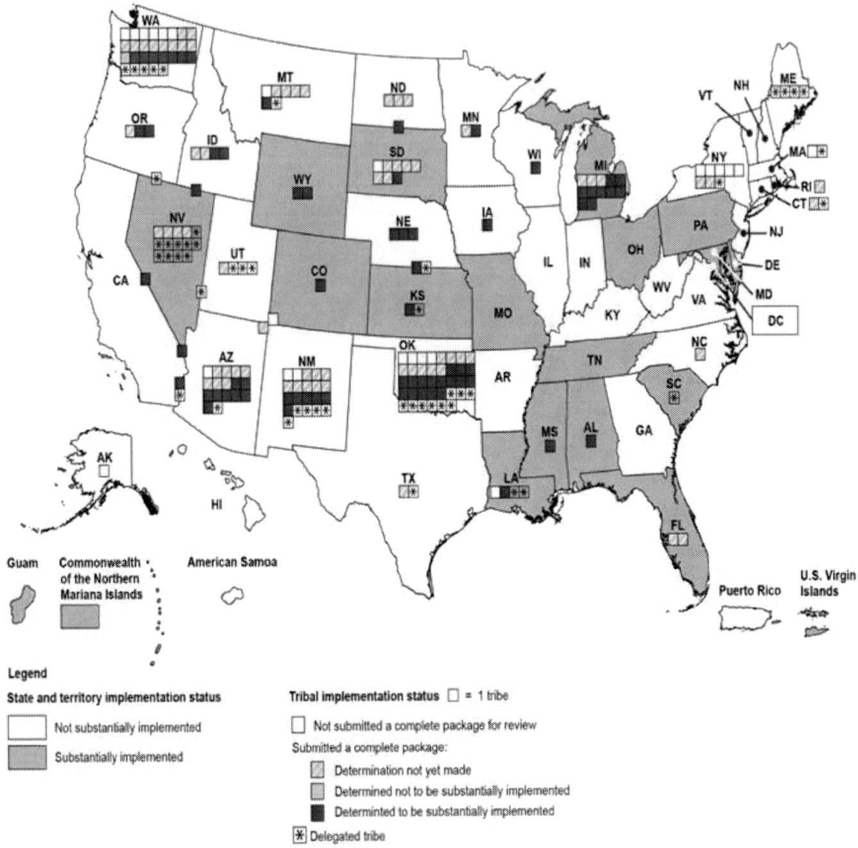

Source: GAO analysis of Office of Sex Offender Sentencing, Montoring, Apprenhending, Registering, and Tracking data; Map Resources (map).| GAO-15-23.

Figure 3. Sex Offender Registration and Notification Act (SORNA) Implementation Status of States and Eligible Tribes, as of August 2014.

According to the SMART Office, the number of tribes that have submitted implementation packages for review as well as the number of tribes that have substantially implemented SORNA continue to increase.

Representatives of two of the three tribal and law enforcement associations we interviewed in January 2014 said that the number of tribes that had substantially implemented SORNA—at the time, 49 tribes—was far greater than what these representatives said that they expected, given the magnitude of the implementation challenges that tribes face, such as limitations with information sharing, a high staff turnover, and the lack of cooperation between tribes and local law enforcement. We discuss such challenges and steps to address them in detail later in this report. According to the tribes that have submitted an implementation package for review that responded to our survey, it took a majority of these tribes 2 years to submit a complete implementation package to the SMART Office for review. SMART Office representatives said that it takes the office, on average, 6 months from the time it receives a tribe's package to begin reviewing it. This is because the office's review depends on a number of factors, such as the availability of SMART Office staff to review implementation packages. At the time of our review, SMART Office representatives indicated that there were three policy advisers on staff to review implementation packages. Additionally, the time it takes for the SMART Office to determine a tribe's implementation status depends on how quickly the tribe can address any issues the SMART Office identifies in its review and can be affected by factors such as the frequency with which a tribal council meets, and thereby can address the office's questions.

Nineteen of the 22 tribes that have not submitted an implementation package responded to our survey and provided a variety of reasons why they have not done so, as well as an estimate of when they expect to do so. Specifically, 7 of the 19 tribes did not submit a package because they are in the process of amending their tribal codes, 4 tribes indicated that they needed additional time to complete and submit their packages, and 3 others either currently have agreements or are in the process of entering into agreements with state and local law enforcement agencies to assist with SORNA implementation.[28]

Fourteen of the 19 tribes plan to submit a package by the end of calendar year 2014, 2 tribes expect to submit a package in calendar year 2015 or later, and 3 tribes are uncertain about when they will submit a package.

SMART Office representatives stated that the office has granted each of these 22 tribes additional time to submit its package. SMART Office representatives said that they have not set a final deadline for tribes to substantially implement SORNA and that the office will continue to work with every tribe that shows interest and is working on implementing the act.

FEDERAL AGENCIES HAVE HELPED TRIBES ADDRESS CHALLENGES, BUT SOME STATES DO NOT NOTIFY TRIBES ABOUT REGISTERED OFFENDERS WHO PLAN TO LIVE, WORK, OR ATTEND SCHOOL ON TRIBAL LAND UPON RELEASE FROM STATE PRISON

About 76 percent of tribes that retained their authority to implement SORNA reported experiencing at least one major or minor challenge to implementing the act. These tribes most frequently reported inability to submit convicted sex offender information to NCIC and NSOR as a major challenge. DOJ and BIA, as well as state and local law enforcement agencies, have taken actions to help address these challenges.

However, additional steps to ensure that states notify tribes about registered sex offenders who plan to live, work, or attend school on tribal lands upon release from state prison, and to identify what, if any, assistance tribes may need in order to implement SORNA, would help further address tribes' challenges.

Tribes Most Frequently Reported Lack of Access to NCIC, Lack of Notification when Convicted Sex Offenders Are Released, and Insufficient Staff

Tribal officials from 98 of the 129 tribes (76 percent) that retained their authority to implement SORNA and responded to our survey questions on challenges to implementing SORNA reported that their tribes experienced at least one major or minor challenge to implementing the act.[29] As shown in figure 4, the major challenges tribes most frequently reported included inability to submit convicted sex offender information to NCIC or NSOR; lack of notification from state prisons about sex offenders who indicate that they plan to live, work, or attend school on tribal lands; insufficient staff; and inability to cover costs to implement SORNA or maintain the tribe's registry.

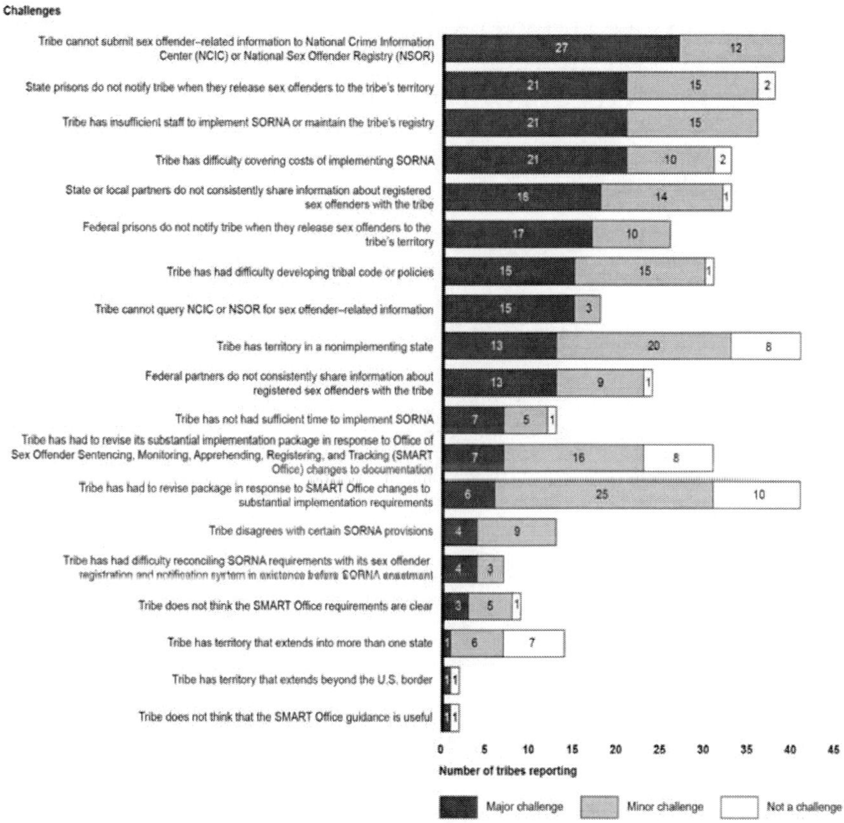

Source: GAO analysis of tribes' survey response.| GAO-15-23.

Note: In our survey, we asked tribes to indicate whether each factor indicated in the graphic applied to their tribe, and if so, whether it was a major, a minor, or not a challenge to SORNA implementation. This graphic does not include the number of tribes that indicated whether or not the factor applied to them. Instead, this graphic includes only the number of tribes that indicated whether the factor was a major or a minor challenge, or not a challenge, to SORNA implementation. The median number of major challenges that tribes reported was 3 and the maximum was 12. In contrast, the median number of minor challenges that tribes reported was 2 and the maximum was 8.

Figure 4. Most Common Factors Tribes Reported to Be a Major Challenge, Minor Challenge, or Not a Challenge to Implementation of the Sex Offender Registration and Notification Act (SORNA).

DOJ and BIA Have Formed a Working Group to Better Coordinate Federal Efforts to Address Tribes' Difficulties Submitting Convicted Sex Offender Information to NCIC or NSOR

Under SORNA, as well as DOJ's National Guidelines for SORNA Implementation, jurisdictions are to provide convicted sex offender information for inclusion in NSOR, which is part of NCIC.[30] However, 39 of the 129 (about 30 percent) tribes that responded to our survey reported difficulties meeting this requirement as a major or minor challenge to SORNA implementation.

These tribes, as well as the federal, state, and tribal sex offender registry and law enforcement officials we interviewed, cited reasons why some tribes do not submit convicted sex offender information to NCIC or are able to do so only with the assistance of other state and local law enforcement agencies.[31]

- *Cost of NCIC access.* Ten tribes that responded to our survey reported that they cannot cover the associated costs for NCIC access. According to federal, state, and tribal officials, these costs can include purchasing servers or NCIC terminals, the cost of the required high-speed Internet connection, or the fees required to obtain NCIC access.
- *Requirements for submitting information to NCIC.* Thirteen tribes reported that they do not meet certain requirements for submitting information to NCIC. CJIS has established requirements that all law enforcement agencies seeking to submit information to federal criminal justice databases must meet in order to ensure the quality and the security of criminal justice data entered into these databases. For example, some tribes do not meet CJIS requirements because they do not have a criminal justice agency (police force, court, etc.) or an officer available 24 hours, 7 days a week to respond to any inquiries about persons or property included in NCIC.
- *State statutes or policies.* Twelve tribes reported that state statutes or policies prevent them from submitting to NCIC through the states' criminal justice information systems. According to FBI officials, CJIS Systems Agencies determine which entities within their states, including tribes, can access these federal criminal databases through state systems. However, some states, such as New York, have statutes or policies prohibiting CSAs from granting tribal law enforcement

entities access to their state switches and, therefore, to NCIC through such switches.[32]

According to DOJ officials, the public safety benefit of including convicted sex offender information in NSOR is that if a law enforcement officer comes into contact with an individual, such as through a traffic stop or an arrest, the officer can query NCIC and learn that the individual is a convicted sex offender and potentially determine if the offender is in compliance with registration requirements. The officer can also enforce any requirements that the officer's jurisdiction may have with regard to convicted sex offenders. For example, according to tribal officials, some tribal jurisdictions banish convicted sex offenders from their lands or prohibit offenders from living or working within proximity to schools or day care centers.

Federal and state, as well as local, law enforcement agencies have undertaken efforts to help address such barriers, although the efforts have some limitations, as discussed below.

Memorandums of agreement (MOA). Federal, state, and local law enforcement agencies have entered into memorandums of agreement with tribes, whereby these law enforcement agencies generally agree to enter convicted sex offender information into NSOR on behalf of the tribes. For example, 28 of 129 (about 22 percent) tribes that responded to our survey reported that county or local law enforcement enters information in NSOR for their tribe, while another 7 tribes indicated that BIA enters this information for them. However, the DOJ and BIA officials and representatives from the National Criminal Justice Association and the National Congress of American Indians that we interviewed noted that not all tribes have good relationships with state or local law enforcement agencies, and that these agencies may not be willing to assist the tribes. In addition, according to DOJ, tribal, and local law enforcement officials, when another law enforcement agency enters information into NSOR on behalf of a tribe, the information is often not associated with the tribe because state or local law enforcement agencies frequently use their own Originating Agency Identifier number (ORI), as opposed to the tribe's number, in NSOR.[33] As a result, the convicted sex offender appears in NSOR as having registered with the entity that submitted the information as opposed to the tribe.

Representatives we interviewed from the SMART Office and CJIS, as well as local and tribal law enforcement, stated that these data entry practices can also lead to imprecise data in NSOR. For example, at our request, CJIS identified 22 tribes as having a total of 247 registered sex offenders in NSOR. However, 120 of 129 tribes that responded to our survey reported that they had a total of 2,167 registered sex offenders on their lands. According to CJIS officials, this discrepancy should not pose a public safety threat because an officer querying an individual in NCIC will know immediately if the individual is a convicted sex offender. Further, CJIS and USMS officials said that the FBI and USMS generally do not use NSOR as their primary source for informing decisions, such as funding or resource allocation for sex offender related operations.

Collaboration to remove state barriers to tribes' NCIC access. The SMART Office has collaborated with state and tribal officials in three states to successfully address state policies preventing tribes in these states from submitting information to NSOR through the state criminal justice database. SMART Office representatives told us that until recently, tribes in Arizona and Washington were unable to submit convicted sex offender information to NSOR because of various state statutes or policies. SMART Office representatives reportedly worked closely with state and tribal officials to provide alternative conduits that will allow tribes to submit convicted sex offender information directly to NSOR. SMART Office representatives also reported that they have tried to persuade officials in at least 2 other states to implement similar solutions, but without success.

Justice Telecommunications System (JUST). DOJ, with the assistance of the Office of Tribal Justice and the Justice Management Division (JMD), established JUST in 2010 as a pilot project to provide tribes that meet FBI requirements with NCIC access. OTJ representatives said that DOJ provided $1 million for the pilot under the Community Oriented Policing Services (COPS) Office and has used approximately $250,000 to provide 21 tribes with NCIC access—6 of which are eligible to implement SORNA.[34] According to OTJ, all tribes that have requested NCIC access through JUST thus far have received access. OTJ representatives said that the JUST funding covers tribes' costs for access fees as well as other licensing and transaction fees; however, tribes will have to pay these fees on their own once the remaining $750,000 for JUST runs out. According to OTJ and JMD representatives, for JUST to become a viable and long-term solution for tribes' lack of NCIC access, DOJ will need to identify and secure a more sustainable source of funding. Identifying sustainable sources of funding, according to these officials, is one of the goals of the Tribal Public Safety Working Group, discussed below.

Tribal Public Safety Working Group. DOJ officials reported that, in addition to the efforts described above, DOJ and BIA established the Tribal Public Safety Working Group in 2014; it consists of representatives from BIA, OTJ, JMD, CJIS, the Office on Violence Against Women, Executive Office for U.S. Attorneys (EOUSA), the SMART Office, and other Office of Justice Programs (OJP) component agencies to identify which tribes lack access to federal databases and to work on the appropriate solution based on the unique circumstances of each tribe.[35] According to OTJ officials, the working group held its kickoff meeting on May 12, 2014, and has established both short-term and long-term goals. In the short term, OTJ representatives said that by using information from outreach efforts and other existing sources, the working group plans to determine the extent to which each tribe has or wants access to all federal criminal databases, and the unique solution based on the circumstances of each tribe. OTJ representatives reported that the working group's long-term goals include identifying sustainable funding sources; identifying best practices for addressing specific barriers; evaluating potential systematic solutions, such as establishing a federal CSA for tribes; and reviewing federal rules and regulations to identify those that should be revised to remove any regulatory barriers to tribes' access to federal criminal databases.

The Tribal Public Safety Working Group's plans and initial activities are in line with addressing the types of barriers to NCIC access that tribes identified. However, given that the Tribal Public Safety Working Group is in its early planning phase, it is too early to evaluate how its efforts will help provide tribes with access to NCIC.

Additional SMART Oversight of, and Outreach to, States Could Help Ensure That Relevant Tribal Jurisdictions Are Notified about Registered Sex Offenders Who Have Indicated That They Will be Moving to Tribal Land upon Release from State Prisons

Of the 129 tribes that responded to our survey, 41 (approximately 32 percent) reported that their state prisons had not notified them when the prisons released a sex offender to the tribes' lands.[36] In addition, about half of these 41 tribes reported that lack of notification when offenders are released from state prisons was a major challenge to SORNA implementation, with some consequences. Tribal officials that we interviewed and that responded to our survey reported instances of offenders on tribal lands that may not be monitored or registered as required because they had not been notified of the offenders' release from prison.[37] For example, one tribal law enforcement official told us that he learned of a convicted sex offender with an extensive criminal record who was released from prison and lived on the tribe's land from anonymous letters the official received. He said that because his tribe received no notification from state prison officials about this sex offender, the sex offender had lived on the tribe's territory unmonitored for over a year.

A consequence of not being notified about registered sex offenders who plan to live, work, or attend school on tribal land upon release from state prisons that tribal officials highlighted was that they may not be able to enforce their own laws governing the extent to which convicted sex offenders can live, work, or attend school in their communities. For example, a state tribal liaison officer told us that 9 of the 29 tribes in his state have laws that ban all sex offenders or restrict the types of sex offenders allowed to live on the tribes' lands. Similarly, officials from 2 tribes we interviewed said that their tribes either did not allow convicted sex offenders to live on the tribes' lands or had more stringent laws than states regarding the proximity of a convicted sex offender's residence to a school. Absent notification from states about registered sex offenders who plan to live, work, or attend school on tribal lands upon release from state prison, tribal authorities would not be aware of the presence of convicted sex offenders on their lands and therefore would be unable to enforce tribal law.

Under SORNA, initial registration of a convicted sex offender is to take place prior to the offender being released from prison, and the registration jurisdiction must immediately forward the offender's registration information to any other jurisdiction in which the sex offender is required to register.[38] However, according to the SMART Office, in many states, the state prison is not a SORNA registering entity and therefore does not register the sex offender or notify other relevant registration jurisdictions prior to the offender's release. In these instances, the sex offender's initial registration may not take place until after the offender is released from prison and through a state registering entity, such as a county sheriff's office. In instances when a sex offender informs a state registering entity—whether that be the state prison, a county sheriff's office, or another agency—that he or she plans to live, work, or attend school on tribal land, under SORNA, notification must be sent to tribes that retained their SORNA implementation authority.[39]

Reasons Why Some States Do Not Notify Tribes

State prison and registry officials who responded to our requests for information provided two reasons why their states do not notify tribes when a registered offender indicates that he or she will be living, working, or attending school on the tribe's land upon release from prison. In some cases, resolving these barriers may be difficult, but in other cases, there are promising practices that could help states to address barriers to notifying tribes. First, 10 of the 20 states that responded to our inquiry said that they do not have laws or policies that require that tribes be notified.[40] Of the 41 tribes that reported that state prisons had not notified them, 22 are located in these states. In the absence of state laws or policies regarding notification to tribes, states may leave it up to the discretion of local law enforcement agencies, which may conduct the initial registration of the sex offender, to decide whether they will notify tribes. However, as discussed earlier, several federal, state, and tribal officials we interviewed acknowledged that not all tribes have cordial relationships with their local law enforcement organizations. As a result, this method of notification may not be effective for all tribes.

Second, it can be difficult for state prisons, in particular, to determine if the address that the offender has identified as that person's residence is located on tribal lands. According to state, local, and tribal officials we interviewed, unlike other jurisdictions, such as cities or counties, tribal lands are not always clearly identifiable by a ZIP code or even a city name. However, the Federal Bureau of Prisons manages this challenge by asking the offender whether the address is located on tribal lands as part of the prison release procedures. In regard to federal notification requirements, officials from the Bureau of Prisons said that they have removed law-enforcement-sensitive information from their notifications. As of May 2014, they can now send prisoner release notifications to both tribal law enforcement and tribal sex offender registry officials to ensure that all tribes are notified when a sex offender is released from federal prison, as required by federal law.[41]

Ensuring Substantially Implemented States Are Notifying Tribes

Of the 30 states that have tribes that retained their authority within their borders, the SMART Office has determined that 10 have substantially implemented SORNA. This means that these states should be notifying tribes; however, 2 of the 10 states are not. In addition, 9 of the 41 tribes located within 6 of the substantially implemented states reported that state prisons had not notified them. Because the SMART Office is responsible for determining the extent to which states are implementing SORNA, it is in a position to verify whether these states are complying with this notification requirement. The SMART Office requires a state to demonstrate how it plans to notify tribes that retained their authority as part of its implementation review.[42] However, the SMART Office granted substantial implementation to 7 states that did not demonstrate how they planned to notify tribes that retained their authority within their borders. SMART Office representatives stated that they granted substantial implementation to these states because, at the time of their review, all or some of the tribes within these states' borders had not yet implemented SORNA. Therefore, these states were unable to provide the SMART Office with plans for how they would notify these tribes until the tribes implemented SORNA themselves.

Also, according to SMART Office representatives, under the flexibility built into SORNA, the SMART Office may determine that a state has substantially implemented the law if lack of notification to tribes was the only area of noncompliance. This is because even though the tribe may not be aware of a convicted sex offender living on its land, it is likely that state or local law enforcement officials have registered and are aware of the sex offender, and can take steps to monitor the offender.[43] However, the SMART Office still expects substantially implemented states to notify tribes following registration of a sex offender who plans to live, work, or attend school on tribal land.

The SMART Office has opportunities to continue to work with substantially implemented states to ensure that they meet this notification requirement. According to SMART Office representatives, the office conducts annual compliance reviews to evaluate the extent to which substantially implemented jurisdictions remain in continued compliance. The office issued its substantial implementation assurance guidance that details the types of information that a SMART Office evaluator is to request when conducting these annual reviews, such as whether the state has signed any new MOAs with tribes. However, the guidance does not require that the evaluator request information on whether and how the state, or a designated agency within the state, notifies tribes following registration of a convicted sex offender who will be, or has recently been, released from state prison and indicates that he or she plans to live, work, or attend school on tribal land. By amending its substantial implementation assurance guidance, the SMART Office could better ensure that substantially implemented states are in compliance with SORNA requirements to notify tribes that retained their authority, thereby enabling these tribes to enforce their own laws pertaining to convicted sex offenders.

Encouraging Nonimplementing States to Notify Tribes

The SMART Office is also in a position to encourage states that have not yet substantially implemented SORNA to make efforts to implement certain provisions of the law, such as the requirement to notify tribes. This is particularly important considering that we found that 7 of 12 nonimplementing states that have tribes that retained their SORNA authority and that responded to our inquiry do not notify tribes. Furthermore, 22 of the 41 tribes that reported state prisons had not notified them are located within these 7 states. The SMART Office has provided guidance and conducted outreach to encourage tribes, once they take responsibility for registering convicted sex offenders, to coordinate with their respective states to ensure that the tribes are notified about sex offenders who plan to live, work, or attend school on their lands upon release from state prison. According to SMART Office representatives, the agency has issued a policies and procedures manual that calls for tribes to, among other things, establish procedures that ensure that the tribe receives notification about a sex offender who is released from a state, county, or local jail, and has indicated that he or she will be living, working, or attending school on tribal land. SMART Office representatives also reported that they have widely encouraged tribes, as a best practice, to contact relevant state, county, and local officials to ensure that these officials are aware that the tribe is a registering jurisdiction and the officials have the tribe's current information on who should receive notifications. SMART Office representatives reported conducting some outreach to states as part of the substantial review process, but acknowledged that more could be done to encourage states to provide notification to tribes. SMART Office representatives said that, prior to our review, they were not aware of tribes' concerns that states were not notifying tribes about sex offenders who were released from prison and planned to live, work, or attend school on tribal lands. Therefore, these representatives did not think it was necessary at the time to provide any additional guidance to the states.

Nevertheless, given our survey results, it may be beneficial for the SMART Office to expand upon its existing outreach efforts to encourage states to develop mechanisms to notify tribes that retained their SORNA implementation authority. SMART Office representatives told us that they often reach out to law enforcement and sex offender registry officials located in both implementing and nonimplementing states and that officials from these states attend various SORNA training events and conferences that the SMART Office sponsors. The representatives agreed that they could use these existing outreach efforts to educate states on the importance of, and best practices for, notifying tribes about sex offenders who have indicated that they plan to live, work, or attend school on tribal lands upon release from state prison. In doing so, the SMART Office will help ensure that implementing, as well as nonimplementing, states have the information they need to effectively notify tribes, and that tribes have the information they need to identify and monitor convicted sex offenders who live, work, or attend school on their lands, and to enforce their laws governing the extent to which convicted sex offenders can live, work, or attend school in their communities.

Additional BIA Outreach to Tribes to Identify the Help They Need and That BIA Can Provide Could Assist Tribes with SORNA Implementation

Insufficient staff and difficulty covering the costs of SORNA implementation were each cited by 21 of 129 (16 percent) tribes as major challenges. Several tribal and federal officials, as well as subject matter experts that we interviewed, also reported that insufficient staff and the costs of SORNA implementation were major challenges that tribes faced when implementing SORNA. For example, BIA and SMART Office representatives and representatives from the National Congress of American Indians told us that because the majority of tribes did not have sex offender registries prior to SORNA, many tribes have not had the necessary resources for conducting sex offender registration, such as office space, staff, and equipment, and therefore would have had to incur significant costs to acquire these resources. In addition, the sex offender registry official from a tribe that has substantially implemented SORNA reported that his tribe spent approximately $173,000 over a period of 2 years to fund his salary, purchase the information technology infrastructure required to set up the tribe's sex offender registry, and acquire a fingerprint scanner. In addition, according to BIA officials and subject matter experts staff turnover can result in large lapses in some tribes' SORNA implementation programs, when staff often leave their positions without providing documentation of past efforts toward implementing the law, requiring incoming staff to start the tribe's implementation efforts anew. For example, according to representatives from the National Criminal Justice Association, 1 tribe has experienced up to six turnovers for its SORNA coordinator position.

DOJ and BIA reported the following as ways in which their agencies have provided tribes with financial assistance, equipment, and staff to help address challenges related to limited resources:

- The SMART Office provided $23.69 million in Adam Walsh Act Implementation Grant Program (AWA) funds to 125 tribes from fiscal years 2008 to 2013 and $1.92 million in Edward Byrne Justice Memorial Discretionary Grants Program funds to 17 tribes in fiscal year 2008 to assist with SORNA implementation.[44]
- The SMART Office also has provided tribes with training and technical assistance related to SORNA implementation as well as numerous tools, including a customizable web-based tool—the Tribe and Territory Sex Offender Registry System (TTSORS)—for tribes to use to set up their sex offender registries and public websites.
- USMS has provided manpower and equipment to assist tribes with conducting operations to ensure convicted sex offenders are complying with their sex offender registration requirements.[45]
- BIA OJS assisted 19 tribes with SORNA implementation tasks, such as providing input on the tribes' draft sex offender codes, assisting tribes with installing or configuring the tribes' registry systems (i.e., TTSORS), and assisting tribes with identifying and implementing alternative means of submitting information to federal criminal databases.

In our survey, 7 tribes reported receiving assistance from BIA, 33 from USMS, and 69 from the SMART Office and almost all of the tribes that reported they received assistance from these three agencies characterized the agencies' assistance as very useful or moderately useful. In addition, tribal leaders we interviewed reported that Byrne and AWA grants have assisted tribes with offsetting the cost of SORNA implementation. Tribal officials responsible for implementing SORNA for 5 tribes reported that their tribes received AWA grant funds and had used the funds to cover various implementation expenses including hiring additional staff, purchasing necessary equipment, and covering fees to query or submit information on convicted sex offenders to federal criminal databases (20 of the 26 tribes that reported challenges with covering SORNA implementation costs and insufficient staff had received AWA grant funds).

A number of tribes that responded to our survey reported that they would like additional assistance from each of the three federal agencies. Specifically,

40 tribes reported that they would like additional assistance from the SMART Office, 30 tribes reported that they would like additional assistance from BIA, and 22 tribes reported that they would like additional assistance from USMS. However, most of the tribes that reported wanting additional assistance from SMART and USMS had already received assistance from these two agencies, and found the assistance to be useful. On the other hand, most of the tribes that reported wanting additional assistance from BIA reported that they had not received any prior assistance from BIA and raised concerns about this. Specifically, 26 tribes that responded to our survey indicated that either BIA did not offer assistance to them at all (14 tribes), they were unsure of the assistance BIA could offer (6 tribes), or that BIA did not provide the assistance they requested (6 tribes). Tribes did not report that the SMART Office or USMS had not offered them assistance or had refused their request for assistance.

Unlike the SMART Office and USMS, BIA does not have an explicit role for SORNA implementation. However, BIA is statutorily responsible for enforcing federal law and, with the consent of the tribe, tribal law in Indian country.[46] Further, the agency is responsible for developing and providing training and technical assistance to tribal law enforcement, and for consulting with tribal leaders to develop regulatory policies and other actions that affect public safety in Indian country— responsibilities that are related to tribes' implementation of SORNA.[47] Moreover, BIA serves as the law enforcement agency for the 40 direct service tribes, 33 of which have retained their authority to implement SORNA.[48]

According to BIA OJS officials, BIA OJS districts have reached out to select tribes that retained their SORNA implementation authority.

However, these officials acknowledged that BIA OJS has not made a concerted effort to offer assistance to all tribes that retained their authority because, according to a senior BIA OJS official, BIA's initial outreach was limited only to tribes that were on a list the agency had received from the SMART Office of tribes that had elected to implement SORNA at the time, and therefore did not include all tribes that subsequently retained their authority to implement.[49] As of July 2013, BIA reported that it had contacted each of the 33 direct service tribes that retained their SORNA implementation authority to determine the tribes' implementation status and what, if any, assistance the tribes would like to have from BIA. BIA OJS reported that the agency provided some form of assistance to 19 of the 33 tribes that the agency contacted. Specifically, BIA OJS reported that it had provided office space to 2 tribes, purchased a fingerprint scanner for another tribe, and assigned officers to 5 tribes to implement or perform some or all aspects of the tribes' sex offender registry and notification systems, and provided technical assistance to the remaining 14 tribes. BIA OJS's officials stated that some tribes refused OJS's offer and others did not respond at all to the offer.[50]

Subsequently, BIA OJS officials reported that the agency conducted another round of outreach to tribes in preparation for a meeting with GAO, in August 2014. However, BIA reached out to only the 33 direct service tribes that had retained their authority but had not yet implemented SORNA and did not contact the remaining 131 tribes that have retained their authority to implement SORNA—71 of which have not yet implemented the law. Furthermore, BIA OJS officials reported that they asked each of the 33 tribes where the tribes were in the implementation process, what challenges they are currently facing, and what if any, assistance BIA had previously offered the tribes, but did not ask what additional help these tribes would like to receive from BIA OJS.

SMART Office representatives said that in addition to tribes' lack of access to NCIC, lack of BIA assistance is the second most frequently reported SORNA implementation challenge that tribes have communicated to the SMART Office. A BIA OJS senior official stated that the agency could better support tribes that choose to retain their SORNA implementation authority, and attributed the agency's challenges in providing this assistance to several factors. First, according to the senior BIA official, tribes experience high staff turnover and incoming staff are often unaware of assistance that BIA may have offered in the past. Therefore, the BIA OJS senior official stated, it is important for BIA to reach out to tribes more than once. Second, the BIA senior official also said that not all BIA field officers have received training on SORNA or how to assist tribes with SORNA implementation. BIA officials said that the agency is working on providing training to its officers so that they have the base knowledge on assisting tribes with SORNA implementation. This training, BIA officials added, will be open to all tribal police chiefs and mandatory for BIA police chiefs.

Third, because BIA conducted outreach to 33 and not all 164 tribes that retained their authority to implement SORNA, BIA may not be aware of the needs of the tribes it has not contacted. BIA officials acknowledged that they could expand their outreach to include all tribes that retained their authority to implement SORNA, including tribes for which the agency does not provide direct services. Taking steps to ascertain what, if any, resource or other needs all tribes that have not implemented SORNA may have could better support the tribes' efforts to substantially implement the act, and thereby better ensure monitoring of convicted sex offenders on tribal lands.

STATES ARE INCLUDING CONVICTED SEX OFFENDERS FROM INELIGIBLE AND DELEGATED TRIBES, BUT STATES ARE NOT CONSISTENTLY NOTIFYING TRIBES ABOUT OFFENDERS WHO INDICATE THAT THEY PLAN TO LIVE, WORK, OR ATTEND SCHOOL ON TRIBAL LANDS

Those states with tribes that are not implementing SORNA—that is, tribes that are not eligible to implement SORNA and tribes whose implementation authority was delegated to a state—reported that the states are including convicted sex offenders on these tribes' lands in the states' own sex offender registration and notification systems. However, states are not consistently notifying these tribes about registered sex offenders who plan to live, work, or attend school on tribal lands upon release from state prison—similar to the problem we discussed earlier that tribes that retained their implementation authority experienced. As a result, some ineligible and delegated tribes are unaware of convicted sex offenders on their lands, in which case they are not able to take actions they deem appropriate to ensure public safety, such as banning certain sex offenders from living on their land.

States Are Including Convicted Sex Offenders from Ineligible and Delegated Tribes in State Registries and Generally Reported No Challenges in Doing So

Under SORNA, states are responsible for registering convicted sex offenders who live, work, or attend school on the territory of tribes that have not retained SORNA implementation authority, which are ineligible tribes subject to state criminal jurisdiction under 18 U.S.C. § 1162, as well as tribes whose SORNA functions have been delegated to a state.[51] We found that states have incorporated ineligible and delegated tribes into state sex offender registries, as required.

With respect to ineligible tribes, we interviewed sex offender registry and SORNA officials in the 6 states where these tribes are located, and they told us that they include convicted sex offenders who live, work, or attend school on tribal lands in the state sex offender registry and had mostly experienced no challenges in doing so. Tribal officials from 7 of 8 ineligible tribes we interviewed confirmed that the states had incorporated convicted sex offenders who live on their lands into the state sex offender registry. An official from the remaining ineligible tribe was not aware of any efforts by the state to include sex offenders who live, work, or attend school on the tribe's land into the state's sex offender registration system.

Officials from 5 of the 6 states where we conducted interviews also reported that their states had experienced no challenges with incorporating convicted sex offenders from ineligible tribes into the state sex offender registry. These state officials reported that for registration purposes, convicted sex offenders on tribal land are required to report to the tribe, a nearby county or city to register. Officials from 3 of the 5 states added that they treat tribes like any other local jurisdiction. Sex offender registry officials we interviewed from the sixth state said that many tribes in their state are located in remote areas, and this poses a challenge for convicted sex offenders located on tribal lands to travel to the nearest county to register. The remote location of these tribes also makes it difficult for county law enforcement to monitor convicted sex offenders to ensure that they are complying with the terms of their registration. According to tribal and sex offender registry officials from this state, the state has tried to address the location challenge by giving offenders who live in remote areas the choice to register in person, by mail or fax and having the tribal community complete forms to verify the addresses of tribal members who are registered sex offenders.

With respect to delegated tribes, SORNA and sex offender registry officials from 10 of the 12 states with these tribes that provided written responses to our questions reported that the states incorporate or expect to incorporate convicted sex offenders from delegated tribes into their state sex offender registry, as required.[52] However, officials from 5 of the 12 states reported difficulties doing so. These included contacting but not receiving a response from tribes and resolving differing requirements between state laws and SORNA regarding registration of sex offenders and community notification. Nevertheless, we found that states were able to overcome these challenges and register and monitor offenders, as required.

States Are Not Consistently Notifying Ineligible and Delegated Tribes about Registered Sex Offenders Who Plan to Live, Work, or Attend School on Tribal Land upon Release from Prison

We reported earlier in this report that some states are not notifying tribes that retained their SORNA implementation authority following registration of a sex offender who plans to live, work, or attend school on tribal land upon release from state prison. Similarly, sex offender registry officials we interviewed from 3 of the 6 states where ineligible tribes are located told us that they do not notify ineligible tribes, and officials from 7 of the 12 states with delegated tribes that responded to our inquiry reported that they also do not notify tribes. Officials from the remaining 3 states where ineligible tribes are located were unsure or did not state whether they notified ineligible tribes while officials from the remaining 5 states with delegated tribes said that they provide tribes with this information.

The specific SORNA provision that requires such notification to ineligible and delegated tribes is section 121(b)(2). It states that immediately after a convicted sex offender registers or updates a registration, an appropriate official in the registration jurisdiction—in this instance, the state—shall provide the information in the registry (other than information exempted from disclosure by the Attorney General) about that offender to all appropriate law enforcement agencies, as well as schools, and public housing agencies, in each area where the offender resides, works, or attends school.[53] Therefore, states should notify all ineligible and delegated tribes that have a law enforcement agency, a school, or a public housing agency when a convicted sex offender registers with the state and plans to live, work, or attend school on tribal land. Of the 50 delegated tribes, 22 have a police department, at least 10 have schools, and 38 have public housing.[54] Similarly, of the 353 ineligible tribes, 17 have their own police department, at least 165 have schools, and 323 have public housing. Yet, states are not consistently notifying these tribes about sex offenders who were released from state prison and registered or updated a registration with the state indicating that they will be living, working, or attending school on tribal lands, as SORNA requires. Without such notification, tribes may be unaware, as noted earlier in this report, of the presence of convicted sex offenders on their lands and may be unable to enforce tribal law and ordinances related to sex offenders.

States are not providing notification to ineligible and delegated tribes that have police departments for a couple of reasons. First, 1 state has determined that tribal law enforcement agencies do not meet the state's definition of a law enforcement agency, in which case the state would not provide this notice. Second, in the absence of state laws or policies to notify tribes, some states let the counties decide on their own whether or not to notify tribal law enforcement, but as we reported earlier in this report, this could be a concern if the tribal and county law enforcement officials do not have a good working relationship.

With respect to the requirement that states notify schools and public housing agencies, the National Guidelines indicate that it is potentially challenging for states to proactively notify schools and public housing agencies because of problems such as identifying comprehensive lists of recipients and maintaining up-to-date contact information for each school and public housing agency. For example, Oklahoma has approximately 1,800 public schools. SMART officials stated that California and Alaska, which have the vast majority of ineligible tribes, might find it particularly challenging. Therefore, the National Guidelines allow states to satisfy the requirement to immediately notify schools and public housing agencies, as well as other community and social service organizations, by posting information on the state's sex offender public website within 3 days of the offender's registration or update, provided that the website includes an automatic notification function whereby requesters may receive e-mails when new information pertaining to a ZIP code or geographic radius area is available.[55] However, this poses challenges. First, tribes can only search by name, ZIP code, county, city or geographic radius, and as we discussed previously, it would be difficult for the tribe to know whether a convicted sex offender who lives within the same ZIP code as the tribe actually lives on tribal land. Second, some states have opted not to include all convicted sex offenders on their public websites, as SORNA allows. For example, jurisdictions can exclude information about tier I offenders whose victims were not minors.[56]

Also, with regard to tribes, an alternative to directly notifying the school or public housing agency located on tribal land could be that the state notify the tribal council or another entity that the tribe deems appropriate. Given the relatively small number of tribes in most states, the number of tribes is likely to be much lower than the number of public housing agencies and schools, making it easier to obtain contact information on tribes and notify them of released offenders. For example, Nevada has 673 public schools, but only 11 delegated tribes, and is the state with the greatest number of delegated tribes. States with ineligible tribes, however, may have a larger number of tribes and find it more difficult to contact each tribe. For example, Alaska and California in particular could find it difficult considering that 226 and 108 ineligible tribes have territory in these states, respectively.

According to the SMART Office, it has taken steps to inform both implementing and nonimplementing states about tribes whose authority has been delegated to the state, and has provided states with points of contact for these tribes. However, the SMART Office has not explicitly advised states, as part of these efforts, to notify delegated tribes about registered sex offenders who intend to live, work, or attend school on tribal land upon release from state prison. Given that the SMART Office conducts annual compliance reviews of implementing states and conducts ongoing outreach to implementing as well as nonimplementing states on a range of SORNA issues, the office is well positioned to provide explicit guidance to states regarding the necessary steps to implement SORNA's notification requirement for ineligible and delegated tribes. Also, through its outreach and compliance reviews, the SMART Office has the opportunity to consult with states on steps they can take to overcome some of the barriers that make it difficult for states to provide these notifications. Such efforts on behalf of the SMART Office would enable ineligible and delegated tribes to take actions they deem necessary to ensure public safety when a convicted sex offender is released from state prison and has registered or updated a registration indicating that he or she will be living, working, or attending school on their lands.

CONCLUSION

SORNA sought to enhance public safety, in part, by requiring eligible tribes to develop their own sex offender registration and notification systems to help address concerns about convicted sex offenders avoiding registration by moving to tribal lands. Considering that many tribes did not have their own sex offender registration systems prior to SORNA, tribes faced a number of challenges in implementing the act, such as lack of access to federal criminal justice databases and difficulty covering implementation costs. Several agencies provided assistance to help tribes address these challenges, but according to tribes that responded to our survey, additional assistance and communication, particularly from BIA, would be beneficial. Also, as part of the SMART Office's annual compliance review of implementing states, and ongoing outreach with implementing and nonimplementing states, determining whether states are notifying tribes that retained their authority about convicted sex offenders who initially register or update a registration indicating that they will be living, working, or attending school on tribal land upon release from state prison could help ensure that tribes are aware of and can monitor convicted sex offenders in their communities. Further, taking additional actions to ensure that states notify all tribes, including ineligible and delegated tribes, would better position tribes to enforce their own laws and policies regarding sex offenders who live, work, or attend school on their land. Further, these actions would enhance DOJ's initiative to increase public safety in tribal communities by providing the federal support these communities need to overcome the unique law enforcement challenges they face, which, as noted by the Attorney General in his 2009 launching of the initiative, had resulted in unacceptable rates of violence against women and children in tribal communities.

RECOMMENDATIONS FOR EXECUTIVE ACTION

To help ensure that tribes that retained their SORNA implementation authority, as well as ineligible and delegated tribes, are notified when convicted sex offenders who intend to live, work, or attend school on tribal land initially register or update a registration, we recommend that the Assistant Attorney General for the Office of Justice Programs direct the SMART Office to take the following two actions:

- Amend its substantial implementation assurance guidance to require its evaluators to determine whether substantially implemented states are notifying tribes that retained their authority to implement SORNA, as well as ineligible and delegated tribes, as required, and use this information in the office's ongoing outreach to the states.
- Encourage implementing as well as nonimplementing states, as part of the office's ongoing outreach to these states, to develop policies and procedures to notify tribes that retained their authority to implement SORNA, as well as ineligible and delegated tribes, about convicted sex offenders who registered or updated a registration with the state—either prior or subsequent to their release from state prison—and indicated that they will be living, working, or attending school on tribal lands. As part of this outreach and to help states overcome any barriers to notifying tribes, educate state officials on best practices for overcoming barriers to notifying tribes that the SMART Office has identified.

To help determine what additional assistance tribes may need to help them toward SORNA implementation, we recommend that the Director of the Bureau of Indian Affairs direct each Office of Justice Services district office to contact the tribes within its district that have retained their implementation authority to determine if the tribes would like BIA to assist them with SORNA implementation efforts. For tribes that would like assistance from BIA, where possible, BIA should provide this assistance or refer the tribe to other resources.

AGENCY COMMENTS AND OUR EVALUATION

We provided a draft of this report to Interior and DOJ for review and comment. We received written comments from DOI via e-mail and from DOJ in a formal letter. DOI and DOJ agreed with our recommendations in their comments. We also received technical comments from DOJ, which are incorporated throughout our report as appropriate.

In comments that DOI provided via e-mail on October 21, 2014, the department agreed with our recommendation that BIA direct each OJS district office to contact the tribes within its district that have retained their implementation authority, to determine if the tribes would like BIA to assist them with SORNA implementation efforts. DOI noted that the department plans to send correspondence to each of these tribes to determine if the tribes need BIA assistance with SORNA implementation and will provide the necessary assistance to these tribes, considering the department's authority, access, and resources. Further, DOI stated that it will reach out to states and other entities outside of OJS's control that may be posing challenges to tribes' ability to comply with SORNA. We believe that these are beneficial steps that, once fully implemented, would address our recommendation and help address resource or other needs that have made it difficult for some tribes to substantially implement the act.

In addition to taking actions to address our recommendation, DOI also identified additional efforts that BIA OJS has under way to help ensure tribes are able to implement SORNA. For example, BIA OJS has renewed its relationship with the SMART Office so as to receive internal policy and procedure updates, as well as training opportunities for OJS employees on SORNA.

DOJ agreed with our recommendation that the SMART Office amend its substantial implementation assurance guidance to require its evaluators to determine whether substantially implemented states are notifying tribes that retained their authority to implement SORNA, as well as ineligible and delegated tribes. The department also noted in its response that the SMART Office will continue to propose individualized solutions for jurisdictions with legislation or public policy practices that inhibit or prohibit working with tribal law enforcement.

DOJ also agreed with our recommendation to encourage implementing as well as nonimplementing states to develop policies and procedures to notify all tribes about sex offenders who would be living, working, or attending school on tribal lands, either prior or subsequent to their release from state prison. In its letter, DOJ noted that the SMART Office will request in future substantial implementation reviews that states provide information on how state incarceration facilities notify tribes when sex offenders are released and have indicated that they will be living, working, or attending school on tribal land. Accordingly, the SMART office will use the information solicited from these reviews in its ongoing outreach to implementing as well as nonimplementing states to help improve their communication with tribes. DOJ stated that to the extent possible, the department will encourage the sharing of sex offender information through the SORNA Exchange Portal—the tool that facilitates the exchange of information about sex offenders moving to other SORNA jurisdictions—as well as through extensive outreach and education to states on how they can use public notification to share information with ineligible and delegated tribes that do not have access to this portal. We believe that, once implemented, these actions would address our recommendations and enhance tribes' ability to receive the notification they need in order to enforce their laws pertaining to sex offenders.

Although DOJ agreed with our recommendations, the department expressed concerns that our report is not responsive to the primary challenge that tribes that responded to our survey identified—that is, an inability to submit sex offender information to federal criminal databases. However, we noted in this report that at the time of our review, DOJ and BIA had established a Tribal Public Safety Working Group to identify which tribes lack access to federal databases and to work on the appropriate solution based on the unique circumstances of each tribe. We believe that it is too soon to evaluate the effectiveness of the working group's current efforts, given that the group is in its early planning phase.

Eileen R. Larence
Director, Homeland Security and Justice Issues

Appendix I. Objectives, Scope, and Methodology

Our objectives for this report were to address the following questions:

- To what extent have eligible tribes retained their authority to implement the Sex Offender Registration and Notification Act (SORNA), and for those that did, what is their implementation status?
- What implementation challenges, if any, have tribes that retained their authority to implement SORNA reported, and what steps have federal agencies and others taken or could take to address these challenges?
- To what extent are states incorporating ineligible and delegated tribes into their state sex offender registration and notification systems?

To address our first two objectives, we surveyed tribal officials whom the Office of Sex Offender Sentencing, Monitoring, Apprehension, Registering, and Tracking (SMART Office) identified as being responsible for implementing the act in the 164 tribes that retained their authority to implement SORNA.[57] These officials included tribal chiefs as well as representatives of tribal police departments and court systems. We used the survey to identify the implementation status of tribes that retained their authority to implement SORNA; the challenges they face with implementation; and the steps that tribes, as well as state, local, and federal government entities, are taking or could take to address implementation challenges. Additionally, we used the survey to obtain the tribal officials' perspectives on the SMART Office's guidance and the criteria it used to determine whether or not a jurisdiction has substantially implemented SORNA. We collaborated closely with a GAO social science survey specialist and conducted an expert review as well as pretests with 4 tribes that retained their authority to implement SORNA; doing so helped us to develop and refine our survey questions, clarify any ambiguous portions of the survey, and identify any potentially biased questions. We launched our web-based survey on April 1, 2014, and closed out the survey on June 30, 2014. Login information for the web-based survey was e-mailed to all participants, and we sent three follow-up e-mail messages to all nonrespondents and contacted the remaining nonrespondents by telephone. We received responses from 80 percent (129 of 161) of all tribes surveyed. Not all survey respondents provided answers to all survey questions.[58] Because the survey was conducted with all tribes that retained their authority to implement SORNA, there are no sampling errors. However, the practical difficulties of conducting any survey may introduce nonsampling errors. For example, differences in how a particular question is interpreted, the sources of information available to respondents, or the types of people who do not respond can introduce unwanted variability into the survey results. We included steps in both the data collection and data analysis stages to minimize such nonsampling errors. We also made multiple contact attempts with nonrespondents during the survey by e-mail and telephone. Since this was a web-based survey, respondents entered their answers directly into the electronic questionnaire, eliminating the need to key data into a database, minimizing error. We examined the survey results and performed computer analyses to identify inconsistencies and other indications of error. A second independent analyst checked the accuracy of all computer analyses.

To address our first objective, we also reviewed the SMART Office's data on eligible tribes' implementation status to identify (1) tribes that have retained their authority to implement SORNA, (2) tribes that have delegated their implementation authority to a state, and (3) tribes whose implementation authority was delegated to a state by the SMART Office. To assess the reliability of the SMART Office's data on tribes' implementation status, we (1) obtained written responses to our questions on how SMART Office representatives who use and maintain the data ensure the data's reliability; (2) checked the data for missing information, and obvious errors; and (3) compared the data regarding tribes' responses against our survey questions regarding their implementation status and, where applicable, interviewed SMART Office officials to determine the reason(s) for and resolve any differences. We found the data to be sufficiently reliable for the purpose of identifying tribes' SORNA implementation status. We also used our survey to determine how long it took tribes to prepare and submit a complete implementation package for SMART Office review, the reasons why some tribes have not submitted a complete package, and when the latter anticipate submitting a complete package.

To address our second objective, we interviewed Department of Justice (DOJ) headquarters officials from the SMART Office, Office of Tribal Justice (OTJ), U.S. Marshals Service (USMS), and the Federal Bureau of Investigation (FBI), as well as Bureau of Indian Affairs (BIA) officials within the Department of the Interior, to determine the implementation challenges tribes have reported and steps the agencies, the tribes, and others have taken to address the challenges. In addition, we interviewed FBI Criminal Justice Information Services Division (CJIS) officials to determine CJIS policies and procedures for granting tribes access to federal criminal justice databases, which are required for SORNA implementation. We also interviewed state, tribal, as well as local law enforcement officials from 5 states—Florida, Michigan, Nevada, New York, and Oklahoma. We selected these 5 states because each contains territory of tribes that retained their authority to implement SORNA and because the states vary with regard to their SORNA implementation status and geographic diversity. In each of the 5 states, we interviewed CJIS System Agency (CSA) officials, the designated state SORNA contact, or state sex offender registry officials to obtain information about state laws, policies, and procedures for granting tribes access to federal criminal justice databases. We also interviewed tribal leaders from 9 eligible tribes in these 5 states—5 of these tribes retained their authority to implement SORNA. We selected the 9 tribes based on factors such as the tribes' implementation status, whether the tribes are direct service tribes, and whether the tribes have agreements for SORNA implementation with any local law enforcement agencies, as well as the challenges that the SMART Office and others reported that these tribes face with implementation.[59] In addition to the 5 states, we contacted officials in 20 states to determine whether these states require their state departments of corrections or registries to notify tribes that have retained their authorities to implement SORNA upon releasing a sex offender who plans to live, work or attend school on tribal lands. Officials from 15 of the 20 states responded to our request. These 15 states plus the 5 we visited included states identified by tribes that responded to our survey as those that do not notify tribes upon releasing sex offenders who plan to live, work, or attend school on tribal lands, as well as states that have substantially implemented SORNA and also have tribes that have retained their authority to implement SORNA. Finally, we interviewed officials from four local law enforcement agencies in proximity to the selected tribes and with whom the tribes had an agreement for SORNA implementation, as well as officials from the two BIA Office of Justice Services (OJS) regional districts with the most direct service tribes that are implementing SORNA to determine what, if any, assistance they have provided the tribes with SORNA implementation. Although the perspectives we obtained from our interviews with these state, BIA, and tribal officials are not generalizable, they provided insights regarding the challenges that tribes face with implementing SORNA and actions that have or could be taken to address the challenges.

We also included questions in our survey of tribes that retained their authority to implement SORNA about the types and extent of challenges the tribes experienced with SORNA implementation; steps the tribes are taking to address the challenges; and the funding and other assistance the tribes have received or could receive from the SMART Office, USMS, BIA, and state or local law enforcement agencies to assist them with implementing the act. In addition, we obtained information from our survey that enabled us to identify tribes that have the required access to the National Crime Information Center (NCIC) and the National Sex Offender Registry (NSOR), and the reasons why some tribes do not have this access.[60] To determine if any improvements are needed to address any of the challenges tribes identified with SORNA implementation, we compared our survey results against SORNA provisions as well as the National Guidelines for Sex Offender Registration and Notification.

To address our third objective, we interviewed state SORNA and sex offender registry officials from all 6 states where ineligible tribes are located as well as 8 ineligible tribes—at least 1 each from these 6 states.

The information from these interviews enabled us to determine if these states include the ineligible tribes in their state SORNA registration and notification systems, as SORNA requires, as well as to identify the challenges, if any, the states and tribes face with having the states implement SORNA on the tribes' behalf. We selected the tribes based on their SORNA implementation status, whether they submitted a resolution to implement SORNA in spite of their ineligibility, and the challenges the tribes reportedly faced with SORNA implementation.[61] We also interviewed tribal leaders from 4 tribes that opted out of SORNA and delegated their registration and notification functions to the state, and solicited responses to written questions from sex offender registry officials in the 15 states to which tribes' authority have been delegated, to determine how states are incorporating delegated tribes into their state sex offender registration and notification systems, as SORNA requires.

To supplement the information we received from our interviews as well as our survey of tribes that retained their SORNA authority, we interviewed officials from three relevant national associations: the National Congress of American Indians, the International Association of Chiefs of Police, and the National Criminal Justice Association, to obtain their perspectives on SORNA eligibility criteria, the SMART Office's delegation criteria and process, the challenges that tribes face with implementation, and the actions that the SMART Office and others have taken to address these challenges. We selected these associations because they represent the interests of tribal communities or state and local law enforcement agencies that assist jurisdictions, including tribes, with SORNA implementation.

We conducted this performance audit from September 2013 to November 2014 in accordance with generally accepted government auditing standards. Those standards require that we plan and perform the audit to obtain sufficient, appropriate evidence to provide a reasonable basis for our findings and conclusions based on our audit objectives. We believe that the evidence obtained provides a reasonable basis for our findings and conclusions based on our audit objectives.

APPENDIX II. SORNA SUBSTANTIAL IMPLEMENTATION CHECKLIST TOOL

The Office of Sex Offender Sentencing, Monitoring, Apprehending, Registering, and Tracking (SMART Office) has developed the Sex Offender Registration and Notification Act (SORNA) Substantial Implementation Checklist tool to be used by jurisdictions in developing, organizing, and submitting a substantial implementation package for review. While not intended to be a definitive guide to SORNA's full implementation requirements, the SORNA checklist is organized into 14 sections covering the major requirements of the law, as shown in table 1.

Table 1. Titles and Descriptions of the 14 Sections of the Sex Offender Registration and Notification Act (SORNA) Substantial Implementation Checklist Tool and Implementation Reports

Section	Basic tenets of covered requirements
I. Immediate Transfer of Information	• Initial and updated registration information must be immediately sent to other jurisdictions where an offender has to register, to relevant federal law enforcement authorities, and to the jurisdiction's public sex offender website.
II. Offenses That Must Be Included in the Registry	• Certain federal, military, and foreign offenses must be included in a jurisdiction's registration scheme, as well as certain sex offenses for which juveniles were adjudicated as delinquent. • A jurisdiction must capture certain sex offenses, both offenses from its jurisdiction and from other SORNA registration jurisdictions, in its registration scheme.
III. Tiering of Offenses	• Offenses must be classified based on the nature of the offense of conviction, established through a baseline three-tier classification system.

Section	Basic tenets of covered requirements
IV. Required Registration Information	• A jurisdiction must collect certain pieces of information from and for each offender that it registers and keep that registration information in a digitized form in its registry.
V. Where Registration Is Required	• A jurisdiction must register an offender if the jurisdiction is the one in which the offender is convicted or incarcerated. In addition, SORNA requires that the jurisdiction register offenders who reside, work, or attend school in the jurisdiction.
VI. Initial Registration: Timing and Notice	• When an offender is incarcerated within the jurisdiction, registration must occur before release from imprisonment. • When an offender is sentenced within the jurisdiction, but not incarcerated, registration must occur within 3 business days of sentencing. • When an offender has been convicted, sentenced, or incarcerated in another jurisdiction (including federal or military court), registration must occur within 3 business days of the offender establishing residence, employment, or school attendance within the jurisdiction. • During initial registration, the offender must be informed of his or her registration duties and acknowledge in writing that he or she understands those duties.

VII. Initial Registration: Retroactive Classes of Offenders	• A jurisdiction must have a procedure in place to recapture three categories of sex offenders:
	  • those currently incarcerated or under supervision,
	  • those already registered or subject to a preexisting registration requirement, and
	  • those who reenter the jurisdiction's criminal justice system because of a conviction for some other felony (whether or not it is a sex offense).

VIII. Keeping the Registration Current	• A registered sex offender must appear in person to update certain changes to required registration information, and must immediately provide changes to other pieces of registration information. • When an offender intends to travel outside the United States, that person must notify the residence jurisdiction at least 21 days in advance. • When a jurisdiction receives notice of an offender's intent to relocate or travel to another country, that jurisdiction must immediately notify any other jurisdiction where the person is required to register, notify the U.S. Marshals, and update the National Sex

Table 1. (Continued)

Section	Basic tenets of covered requirements
	Offender Registry within the National Crime Information Center.
IX. Verification/ Appearance Requirements	• Offenders must register for a duration of time and make in-person appearances at the registering agency based on the tier of the offense of conviction.
X. Registry Website Requirements	• A jurisdiction must maintain a public sex offender registry website and publish certain registration information on that website, such as the offender's name, address information, the sex offense for which the offender is registered, and a current photograph. • Certain information must not be displayed on a jurisdiction's public registry website, such as the offender's Social Security number or the identity of the victim.
XI. Community Notification	• A jurisdiction must disseminate certain initial and updated registration information to (1) particular agencies within the jurisdiction and (2) the community.
XII. Failure to Register as a Sex Offender: State Penalty	• Each jurisdiction, other than a federally recognized Indian tribe, must provide a criminal penalty that includes a maximum term of imprisonment that is greater than 1 year for the failure of a sex offender to comply with its registration requirements.
XIII. When Sex Offender Fails to Appear for Registration	• When a jurisdiction is notified that a sex offender intends to reside, be employed, or attend school in its jurisdiction, and that offender fails to appear for registration as required, the jurisdiction receiving that notice must inform the originating jurisdiction (the jurisdiction that provided the initial notification) that the sex offender failed to appear for registration.
XIV. When a Jurisdiction Has Information that a Sex Offender May Have Absconded	• When a jurisdiction has information that a sex offender may have absconded, the jurisdiction must take certain actions to investigate the absconder and notify various law enforcement agencies.

Source: Department of Justice: Office of Sex Offender Sentencing, Monitoring, Apprehending, Registering, and Tracking (SMART Office) | GAO-15-23.

Note: If a state has a tribe or tribes located within its boundaries that have elected to implement SORNA, the SMART Office also requests that these states provide additional information, such as an explanation of the working relationship with the relevant SORNA tribe(s), when submitting a substantial implementation package for review.

APPENDIX III. EXTENT TO WHICH ELIGIBLE TRIBES HAVE IMPLEMENTED THE SEX OFFENDER REGISTRATION AND NOTIFICATION ACT (SORNA)

According to the Office of Sex Offender Sentencing, Monitoring, Apprehending, Registering, and Tracking (SMART Office), the 214 tribes that are eligible to implement SORNA are located in 33 states; of these states, 11 have substantially implemented SORNA. As of August 2014, the SMART Office has determined that 164 tribes have retained their authority to implement SORNA, while the remainder did not retain their authority because they either elected to delegate their authority to a state (24 tribes) or the SMART Office delegated their authority to a state (26 tribes). Of the tribes that have retained their authority to implement the act, 71 tribes have substantially implemented SORNA; 70 tribes have submitted a complete package, but the SMART Office has not yet made a determination; 22 tribes have not submitted a complete package; and 1 tribe has not substantially implemented the act.

Table 2. Implementatlon Status of Eligible Tribes and Their Corresponding States, as of August 2014

State	Number of tribes	Tribe	Implementation authority	SORNA implementation status
Alabama	1			●
		Poarch Band of Creeks	Retained authority	●
Alaska	1			□
		Metlakatla Indian Com€munity	Retained authority	‡
Arizona	21			□
		Ak-Chin Indian Community Council	Retained authority	ஒ
		Cocopah Tribal Council	Retained authority	ஒ

Table 2. (Continued)

State	Number of tribes	Tribe	Implementation authority	SORNA implementation status
		*Colorado River Indian Tribes	Retained authority	•
		Fort McDowell Yavapai Nation	Retained authority	•
		~*Fort Mojave Indian Tribe	Retained authority	•
		Gila River Indian Community	Retained authority	•
		Havasupai Tribe	Retained authority	δl
		Hopi Tribe	Retained authority	•
		Hualapai Indian Tribe	Retained authority	•
		Kaibab Band of Paiute Indians	Retained authority	δl
		~ Navajo Nation	Retained authority	δl
		Pascua Yaqui Tribe	Retained authority	•
		*Quechan Tribe of the Fort Yuma Indian Reservation	Delegated (SMART)	n/a
		Salt River Pima-Maricopa Indian Community	Retained authority	•
		San Carlos Apache Tribe	Retained authority	‡
		San Juan Southern Paiute tribe of Arizona	Delegated Office of Sex Offender Sentencing, Monitoring, Apprehending, Registering, and Tracking (SMART Office)	n/a
		Tohono O'odham Nation	Retained authority	•
		Tonto Apache Tribe	Retained authority	δl
		White Mountain Apache Tribe	Retained authority	δl

State	Number of tribes	Tribe	Implementation authority	SORNA implementation status
		Yavapai-Apache Nation	Retained authority	●
		Yavapai-Prescott Indian Tribe	Retained authority	⊙
Colorado	2			●
		Southern Ute Indian Tribe	Retained authority	●
		~ Ute Mountain Ute Tribe	Retained authority	‡
Connecticut	2			□
		Mashantucket Pequot Indian Tribe	Retained authority	ᘰ
		Mohegan Indian Tribe of Connecticut	Delegated (Tribe)	n/a
Florida	2			●
		Miccosukee Indian Tribe	Retained authority	ᘰ
		Seminole Tribe of Florida	Retained authority	ᘰ
Idaho	5			□
		Coeur D'Alene Tribe	Retained authority	ᘰ
		Kootenai Tribe of Idaho	Retained authority	●
		Nez Perce Tribe	Retained authority	ᘰ
		Shoshone-Bannock Tribes of the Fort Hall Reservation	Retained authority	●
		~ Shoshone-Paiute Tribes of the Duck Valley Reservation	Retained authority	●
Iowa	1			□
		Sac & Fox Tribe of the Mississippi in Iowa	Retained authority	●

Table 2. (Continued)

State	Number of tribes	Tribe	Implementation authority	SORNA implementation status
Kansas	4			●
		*Iowa Tribe of Kansas & Nebraska	Retained authority	●
		Kickapoo Tribe of Indians of the Kickapoo Reservation in Kansas	Delegated (Tribe)	n/a
		Prairie Band of Potawatomi Nation	Retained authority	●
		*Sac and Fox Nation of Missouri in Kansas and Nebraska	Delegated (SMART)	n/a
Louisiana	4			●
		Chitimacha Tribe of Louisiana	Retained authority	●
		Coushatta Tribe of Louisiana	Delegated (Tribe)	n/a
		Jena Band of Choctaw Indians	Delegated (Tribe)	n/a
		Tunica-Biloxi Tribe	Retained authority	‡
Maine	4			□
		Aroostook Band of Micmacs	Delegated (SMART)	n/a
		Houlton Band of Maliseet Indians	Delegated (Tribe)	n/a
		Passamaquoddy Tribe	Delegated (SMART)	n/a
		Penobscot Indian Nation	Delegated (SMART)	n/a
Massachusetts	2			□
		Mashpee Wampanoag Tribe	Delegated (Tribe)	n/a

State	Number of tribes	Tribe	Implementation authority	SORNA implementation status
		Wampanoag Tribe of Gay Head / Aquinnah	Retained authority	‡
Michigan	12			•
		Bay Mills Indian Community	Retained authority	•
		Grand Traverse Band of Ottawa and Chippewa Indians	Retained authority	•
		Hannahville Indian Community	Retained authority	•
		Keweenaw Bay Indian Community	Retained authority	•
		Lac Vieux Desert Band of Lake Superior Chippewa Indians	Retained authority	ฤ
		Little River Band of Ottawa Indians	Retained authority	ฤ
		Little Traverse Bay Bands of Odawa Indians	Retained authority	•
		Match-e-be-nash-she-wish Band of Pottawatomi Indians of Michigan	Retained authority	•
		Nottawaseppi Huron Band of the Potawatomi	Retained authority	•
		Pokagon Band of Potawatomi Indians	Retained authority	ฤ
		Saginaw Chippewa Indian Tribe of Michigan	Retained authority	•
		Sault Ste. Marie Tribe of Chippewa Indians of Michigan	Retained authority	•

Table 2. (Continued)

State	Number of tribes	Tribe	Implementation authority	SORNA implementation status
Minnesota	2			□
		Minnesota Chippewa Tribe Bois Forte Band	Retained authority	●
		Red Lake Band of Chippewa Indians of Minnesota	Retained authority	δl
Mississippi	1			●
		Mississippi Band of Choctaw Indians	Retained authority	●
Montana	7			□
		Assiniboine and Sioux Tribes of the Fort Peck Indian Reservation	Retained authority	δl
		Blackfeet Tribe of the Blackfeet Indian Reservation of Montana	Retained authority	‡
		Chippewa Cree Tribe of the Rocky Boy's Reservation	Retained authority	●
		Confederated Salish & Kootenai Tribes of the Flathead Reservation	Delegated (Tribe)	n/a
		Crow Tribe of Montana	Retained authority	δl
		Fort Belknap Indian Community of the Fort Belknap Reser-vation of Montana	Retained authority	δl
		Northern Cheyenne Tribe	Retained authority	δl
Nebraska	3			□
		Omaha Tribe of Nebraska	Retained authority	●
		Santee Sioux Nation	Retained authority	●
		Winnebago Tribe of Nebraska	Retained authority	●

State	Number of tribes	Tribe	Implementation authority	SORNA implementation status
Nevada	19			•
		~Confederated Tribes of Goshute Reservation	Delegated (SMART)	n/a
		Duckwater Shoshone Tribe	Delegated (Tribe)	n/a
		Ely Shoshone Tribe of Nevada	Retained authority	♌
		*Fort McDermitt Paiute & Shoshone Tribes of the Fort McDermitt Indian Reservation	Delegated (SMART)	n/a
		~*Fort Mojave Indian Tribe	Retained authority	•
		Las Vegas Tribe of the Paiute Indians of the Las Vegas Colony	Delegated (SMART)	n/a
		Lovelock Paiute Tribe of the Lovelock IndianColony	Delegated (SMART)	n/a
		Moapa Band of Paiute Indians of the Moapa River Indian eservation	Delegated (SMART)	n/a
		Paiute-Shoshone Tribe of the Fallon Reservation and Colony	Delegated (SMART)	n/a
		Pyramid Lake Paiute Tribe	Retained authority	♌
		Reno-Sparks Indian Colony	Retained authority	♌
		~Shoshone-Paiute Tribes of the Duck Valley Reservation	Retained authority	•
		Summit Lake Paiute Tribe	Delegated (SMART)	n/a

Table 2. (Continued)

State	Number of tribes	Tribe	Implementation authority	SORNA implementation status
		Te-Moak Tribe of Western Shoshone Indians of Nevada	Retained authority	ᶋ
		Walker River Paiute Tribe	Delegated (Tribe)	n/a
		*Washoe Tribe of Nevada and California	Retained authority	●
		Winnemucca Indian Colony of Nevada	Delegated (SMART)	n/a
		Yerington Paiute Tribe	Delegated (SMART)	n/a
		Yomba Shoshone Tribe	Delegated (SMART)	n/a
New Mexico	23			□
		Jicarilla Apache Nation	Retained authority	●
		Kewa Pueblo (Pueblo of Santo Domingo)	Retained authority	ᶋ
		Mescalero Apache Tribe	Retained authority	●
		Ohkay Owingeh	Retained authority	●
		Pueblo of Acoma	Retained authority	●
		Pueblo of Cochiti	Retained authority	ᶋ
		Pueblo of Isleta	Retained authority	●
		Pueblo of Jemez	Retained authority	ᶋ
		Pueblo of Laguna	Retained authority	ᶋ
		Pueblo of Nambe	Delegated (Tribe)	n/a
		Pueblo of Picuris	Delegated (SMART)	n/a
		Pueblo of Pojoaque	Delegated (Tribe)	n/a
		Pueblo of San Felipe	Retained authority	‡
		Pueblo of San Ildefonso	Retained authority	ᶋ
		Pueblo of Sandia	Delegated (Tribe)	n/a
		Pueblo of Santa Ana	Retained authority	●
		Pueblo of Santa Clara	Retained authority	ᶋ
		Pueblo of Taos	Retained authority	ᶋ

State	Number of tribes	Tribe	Implementation authority	SORNA implementation status
		Pueblo of Tesuque	Retained authority	‡
		Pueblo of Zia	Delegated (SMART)	n/a
		~ Navajo Nation	Retained authority	ߍ
		~ Ute Mountain Ute Tribe	Retained authority	‡
		Zuni Tribe of the Zuni Reservation (Pueblo Zuni)	Retained authority	ߍ
New York	8			⊓
		Cayuga Nation	Retained authority	◊
		Oneida Nation of New York	Retained authority	ߍ
		Onondaga Nation	Retained authority	‡
		Saint Regis Mohawk Tribe	Retained authority	ߍ
		Seneca Nation of Indians	Delegated (Tribe)	n/a
		Shinnecock Indian Nation	Retained authority	‡
		Pawnee Nation of Oklahoma	Retained authority	‡
		Peoria Tribe of Indians of Oklahoma	Retained authority	ߍ
		Ponca Tribe of Indians of Oklahoma	Delegated (Tribe)	n/a
		Quapaw Tribe of Indians	Retained authority	ߍ
		Sac and Fox Nation	Retained authority	ߍ
		Seminole Nation of Oklahoma	Retained authority	•
		Seneca-Cayuga Tribe of Oklahoma	Retained authority	•
		Shawnee Tribe	Delegated (SMART)	n/a
		Thlopthlocco Tribal Town	Delegated (Tribe)	n/a
		Tonkawa Tribe of Indians of Oklahoma	Retained authority	ߍ

Table 2. (Continued)

State	Number of tribes	Tribe	Implementation authority	SORNA implementation status
		United Keetoowah Band of Cherokee Indians in Oklahoma	Retained authority	●
		Wichita and Affiliated Tribes	Delegated (SMART)	n/a
		Wyandotte Nation	Retained authority	●
Oregon	3			□
		Burns Paiute Tribe	Retained authority	ᕳ
		Confederated Tribes of the Umatilla Indian Reservation	Retained authority	●
		Confederated Tribes of the Warm Springs Reservation	Retained authority	●
Rhode Island	1			□
		Narragansett Indian Tribe	Retained authority	ᕳ
South Carolina	1			●
		Catawba Indian Nation	Delegated (SMART)	N/A
South Dakota	9			●
		Cheyenne River Sioux Tribe of the Cheyenne River Reservation	Retained authority	ᕳ
		Crow Creek Sioux Tribe of the Crow Creek Reservation	Retained authority	ᕳ
		Flandreau Santee Sioux Tribe of South Dakota	Retained authority	ᕳ
		Lower Brule Sioux Tribe of the Lower Brule Reservation	Retained authority	ᕳ
		Oglala Sioux Tribe	Retained authority	ᕳ

State	Number of tribes	Tribe	Implementation authority	SORNA implementation status
		Rosebud Sioux Tribe	Retained authority	δl
		Sisseton - Wahpeton Oyate of the Lake Traverse Reservation	Retained authority	●
		~ Standing Rock Sioux Tribe	Retained authority	●
		Yankton Sioux Tribe of South Dakota	Retained authority	δl
Texas	2			□
		Alabama-Coushatta Tribes of Texas	Retained authority	δl
		Ysleta del Sur Pueblo of Texas	Delegated (Tribe)	n/a
Utah	7			□
		~ Confederated Tribes of Goshute Reservation	Delegated (SMART)	n/a
		~ Navajo Nation	Retained authority	δl
		Northwestern Band of Shoshone Nation	Delegated (Tribe)	n/a
		Paiute Indian Tribe of Utah	Delegated (SMART)	n/a
		Skull Valley Band of Goshute Indians	Delegated (Tribe)	n/a
		Ute Indian Tribe	Retained authority	δl
		~ Ute Mountain Ute Tribe	Retained authority	‡
Washington	29			□
		Confederated Tribes and Bands of the Yakama Nation	Retained authority	●
		Confederated Tribes of the Chehalis Reservation	Retained authority	□
		Confederated Tribes of the Colville Reservation	Retained authority	δl

Table 2. (Continued)

State	Number of tribes	Tribe	Implementation authority	SORNA implementation status
		Cowlitz Indian Tribe	Delegated (Tribe)	n/a
		Hoh Indian Tribe	Delegated (Tribe)	n/a
		Jamestown S'Klallam Tribe	Delegated (Tribe)	n/a
		Kalispel Tribe of Indians	Retained authority	●
		Lower Elwha Klallam Tribe	Retained authority	●
		Lummi Tribe of the Lummi Reservation	Retained authority	ᶋ
		Makah Indian Tribe of the Makah Indian Reservation	Retained authority	ᶋ
		Muckleshoot Indian Tribe	Retained authority	‡
		Nisqually Indian Tribe	Retained authority	‡
		Nooksack Indian Tribe	Retained authority	ᶋ
		Port Gamble S'Klallam Tribe	Retained authority	ᶋ
		Puyallup Tribe of the Puyallup Reservation	Retained authority	ᶋ
		Quileute Tribe	Retained authority	‡
		Quinault Indian Nation	Retained authority	●
		Samish Indian Nation	Retained authority	◊
		Sauk-Suiattle Indian Tribe	Retained authority	ᶋ
		Shoalwater Bay Indian Tribe	Retained authority	ᶋ
		Skokomish Indian Tribe	Retained authority	●
		Snoqualmie Indian Tribe	Delegated (Tribe)	n/a
		Spokane Tribe of the Spokane Reservation	Retained authority	●

State	Number of tribes	Tribe	Implementation authority	SORNA implementation status
		Squaxin Island Tribe	Retained authority	ᘐ
		Stillaguamish Tribe of Indians of Washington	Delegated (Tribe)	n/a
		Suquamish Indian Tribe of the Port Madison Reservation	Retained authority	ǂ
		Swinomish Indian Tribal Community	Retained authority	ᘐ
		Tulalip Tribes of Washington	Retained authority	ᘐ
		Upper Skagit Indian Tribe	Retained authority	●
Wisconsin	1			□
		Menominee Indian Tribe of Wisconsin	Retained authority	●
Wyoming	2			●
		Arapaho Tribe of the Wind River Reservation	Retained authority	●
		Shoshone Tribe of the Wind River Reservation	Retained authority	●

Source: GAO analysis of SMART Office data | GAO-15-23

Legend:

n/a = not applicable.

*Tribe = the tribe has territory in another state, but is ineligible to implement SORNA in that state.

~Tribe = the tribe has territory in multiple states and is eligible to implement SORNA in each of those states. Thus, the tribe is represented under multiple states.

● = Substantially implemented

ᘐ= Submitted a complete package, determination not yet made

□ = Not substantially implemented

ǂ= Not submitted a complete package for review

◊ = Held in abeyance

Δ = Newly recognized tribes

End Notes

[1] The Jacob Wetterling Crimes Against Children and Sexually Violent Offender Registration Act (Wetterling Act), Pub. L. No. 103-322, tit. XVII, subtit. A, 108 Stat. 1796, 2038-42 (1994), provided a national baseline for sex offender registration programs. This affected matters such as defining the offenses that require registration and the duration of registration periods, requiring periodic verification of the registered address, continued registration of sex offenders when they move from one state to another (if the new state had a registration requirement), and community notification. In the years subsequent to the enactment of the Wetterling Act, Congress passed a series of amendments to this federal legislation, which in part reflected and promoted trends and developments in individual states' registration programs. Key legislative amendments were enacted by Megan's Law, Pub. L. No. 104-145, 110 Stat. 1345 (1996); the Pam Lychner Sexual Offender Tracking and Identification Act of 1996, Pub. L. No. 104-236, 110 Stat. 3093; the Jacob Wetterling Improvements Act, Pub. L. No. 105-119, § 115, 111 Stat. 2440, 2461-67 (1997); Protection of Children from Sexual Predators Act, of 1998, Pub. L. No. 105-314, 112 Stat. 2974; the Campus Sex Crimes Prevention Act, Pub. L. No. 106-386, § 1601, 114 Stat. 1464, 1537-38 (2000); and the Prosecutorial Remedies and Other Tools to End the Exploitation of Children Today (PROTECT) Act, Pub. L. No. 108-21, 117 Stat. 650 (2003).

[2] Pub. L. No. 109-248, tit. I, 120 Stat. 587, 590-607 (2006).

[3] See 42 U.S.C. § 16924(b).

[4] 42 U.S.C. § 16927(a)(1), (a)(2)(A). Federally recognized tribes are eligible to receive federal funding and services. Under 42 U.S.C. § 16927(a)(2)(A), tribes that are subject to the criminal jurisdiction of a state under 18 U.S.C. § 1162 are not eligible to implement the act. Tribes subject to state criminal jurisdiction under section 1162 are located in 6 states: California, Minnesota, Nebraska, Oregon, Wisconsin, and Alaska. In addition, the Kickapoo Traditional Tribe of Texas is also subject to state criminal jurisdiction pursuant to section 1162 and is therefore ineligible to implement SORNA. See 25 U.S.C. § 1300b-15.

[5] GAO, *Sex Offender Registration and Notification Act: Jurisdictions Face Challenges to Implementing the Act, and Stakeholders Report Positive and Negative Effects,* GAO-13-211 (Washington, D.C.: Feb. 7, 2013).

[6] Pursuant to section 127 of SORNA, designated federally recognized Indian tribes were entitled to elect to become SORNA registration and notification jurisdictions or to delegate the responsibility to the jurisdiction or jurisdictions within which the territory of the tribe is located. See 42 U.S.C. § 16927(a)(1).

[7] 42 U.S.C. § 16927(a)(2).

[8] At the time of our survey, 166 tribes had retained their authority to implement SORNA. We did not survey 5 of the 166 because, according to the SMART Office, these tribes are either newly recognized tribes and have not elected whether or not they want to implement SORNA, or are still in the process of acquiring land. These tribes include the Cayuga Nation, the Delaware Tribe of Indians, the Samish Indian Nation, and the Shinnecock Indian Nation. We also did not survey the Onondaga Indian Nation because tribal officials told us that at the time of our survey they were in the process of delegating their SORNA authority to the state and had not taken any actions to implement the act. For more details of our survey results see GAO, *Sex Offender Registration and Notification Act: Survey of Federally Recognized Tribes on Implementation of the Act (*GAO-15-30SP, November 2014), an E-supplement to GAO-15-23, (Washington, D.C.: Nov. 18, 2014).

[9] USMS is responsible for locating and apprehending noncompliant convicted sex offenders, while the FBI is responsible for operating the National Sex Offender Registry, the database for registering convicted sex offenders.

[10] The Bureau of Indian Affairs provides direct services, such as law enforcement services, to certain tribes, commonly referred to as direct service tribes, that do not operate certain programs themselves. See 25 U.S.C. §§ 450f, 2802(c)(1).

[11] 73 Fed. Reg. 38,030 (July 2, 2008). DOJ issued these guidelines in support of jurisdictions' efforts to implement the act. The guidelines outline measures jurisdictions must implement in order for the agency to determine that they have "substantially implemented" SORNA.

[12] SORNA required eligible tribes wishing to implement the act to submit a resolution within a year of the act's enactment, electing to implement the law themselves as opposed to delegating their authority to implement to a state. 42 U.S.C. § 16927(a)(1)(A), (a)(2)(B).

[13] Under SORNA, a convicted sex offender must be informed of his or her registration obligations, initial registration shall take place prior to the offender being released from prison, and registration information is to be immediately forwarded to any other jurisdiction in which the sex offender is required to register. 42 U.S.C. §§ 16911(10)(H), 16913(b)(1), 16917(a), 16921(b). Sex offenders who are not sentenced to a term of imprisonment are to register not later than 3 business days after being sentenced. 42 U.S.C. § 16913(b)(2).

[14] For the standards described in this paragraph, see 42 U.S.C. §§ 16911-16913, 16915- 16916, 16918.

[15] NCIC is a computerized index of criminal justice information (i.e., fugitives, stolen properties, and missing persons) that is available to authorized federal, state, local, territorial, and tribal law enforcement and other criminal justice agencies 24 hours a day, throughout the year. NSOR is a national database within NCIC that authorized federal, state, local, territorial, and tribal law enforcement officials can use to access information on registered sex offenders throughout the United States.

[16] IAFIS is a national automated fingerprint identification and criminal history system maintained by the FBI that provides automated fingerprint search capabilities, electronic image storage, and electronic exchange of fingerprints. CODIS, also maintained by the FBI, is a multilevel database where DNA profiles can be stored and searched. The FBI's National Palm Print System is a centralized repository for palm print data that law enforcement can access nationwide to solve crimes.

[17] A CSA is the agency responsible for the administration and usage of the CJIS Division Programs for a state.

[18] 42 U.S.C. § 16921(b). SORNA defines *jurisdiction* as any of the 50 states, the District of Columbia, Puerto Rico, Guam, American Samoa, the Northern Mariana Islands, the U.S. Virgin Islands, and federally recognized tribes implementing SORNA under 42 U.S.C. § 16927. See 42 U.S.C. § 16911(10).

[19] The sum total of eligible tribes (214) and ineligible tribes (353) is 1 tribe greater than the total number of federally recognized tribes (566) because the Minnesota Chippewa Tribe, for SORNA purposes, was split into two eligibility categories. One component of the tribe—the Bois Forte Band (Nett Lake)—became eligible because the state retroceded jurisdiction to this band only, while other components of the tribe remained ineligible.

[20] See 42 U.S.C. § 16927(a)(2)(A).

[21] 18 U.S.C. § 1162(a). Section 1162, however, does not give the state criminal jurisdiction over the Red Lake Reservation of Minnesota, the Warm Springs Reservation of Oregon, and the Metlakatla Indian Community of the Annette Islands Reservation in Alaska. In addition to these three statutory exceptions, the Secretary of the Interior is authorized to accept retrocession of jurisdiction by a state. See 25 U.S.C. § 1323(a). For example, Wisconsin retroceded state jurisdiction over the Menominee Reservation pursuant to the Menominee Restoration Act, Pub. L. No. 93-197, 87 Stat. 770 (1973) (codified at 25 U.S.C. §§ 903-903f); Menominee Indian Reservation in Wisconsin; Acceptance of Offer to Retrocede Jurisdiction, 41 Fed. Reg. 8516 (Feb. 27, 1976); *State v. Webster*, 338 N.W.2d 474, 476-77 (Wis. 1983). Accordingly, the tribes located on these reservations, as well as tribes subject to retrocession of state criminal jurisdiction, are eligible to implement SORNA. The Kickapoo Traditional Tribe of Texas is also subject to state criminal jurisdiction in

accordance with section 1162, and is therefore ineligible to implement SORNA. See 25 U.S.C. § 1300b-15.

[22] 42 U.S.C. § 16927(a).

[23] 42 U.S.C. § 16945.

[24] See 76 Fed. Reg. 1630, 1636-39 (Jan. 11, 2011).

[25] Under the Indian Self-Determination and Education Assistance Act of 1975, as amended, federally recognized tribes can enter into self-determination contracts and self- governance compacts with the federal government to take over administration of certain federal programs previously administered on their behalf. Pub. L. No. 93-638, 88 Stat. 2203 (codified as amended at 25 U.S.C. §§ 450-458ddd-2). Self-determination contracts allow tribes to assume responsibility for managing the program's day-to-day operations, with BIA providing technical oversight to ensure that the tribe meets contract terms, as opposed to BIA administering the program on their behalf. Self-governance compacts transfer to tribes the administration of the program and provide the tribes with some flexibility in program administration. For both self-determination contracts and self- governance compacts, the Secretary of the Interior negotiates and enters into written annual funding agreements with the governing body of the tribe, which specifies the Interior program that the tribe will administer, the tribe's and Interior's obligations, and the funds being transferred to the tribe.

[26] We selected 2 tribes from the states we had already selected for our review. We did not interview the remaining 22 tribes.

[27] SORNA requires law enforcement officials to continually monitor registered sex offenders to ensure that offenders comply with the terms of their registration. See 42 U.S.C. §§ 16916, 16922. Where offenders are located in areas considered as remote, this may pose access challenges for monitoring officials.

[28] Additional reasons why tribes did not submit a package included staff turnover (2 tribes), lack of cooperation from federal or state partners (2 tribes), and prioritizing other law enforcement issues (1 tribe).

[29] Our survey presented a list of 19 factors that could pose a challenge to tribes' implementation of SORNA. For each factor, we asked tribes to check whether the factor applied to them, and if so, if it posed a major challenge, a minor challenge, or no challenge to SORNA implementation. We also provided tribes the opportunity to identify other challenges in an open comment box.

[30] 42 U.S.C. §§ 16919, 16921(b)(1)

[31] Of the tribes that responded to our survey, 58 reported that they are able to submit sex offender information to NSOR, but only with the assistance of another federal, state, or local law enforcement agency. They are not able to submit this information on their own.

[32] See, e.g., N.Y. Crim. Proc. Law § 1.20(34) (McKinney 2014) (tribal law enforcement officers are not specifically listed as persons considered "police officers" under New York law). State switches enable access to federal and state databases.

[33] FBI CJIS assigns an Originating Agency Identification number to each agency that it has granted access to federal criminal databases so as to easily link the information to a particular agency.

[34] The COPS Office is a DOJ component agency that seeks to advance the practice of community policing in state, local, and tribal law enforcement agencies. COPS does its work principally by sharing information and making grants to police departments around the United States.

[35] The Office on Violence Against Women, a component of DOJ, is responsible for providing federal leadership in developing the national capacity to reduce violence against women and administer justice for and strengthen services to victims of domestic violence, dating violence, sexual assault, and stalking. The Office of Justice Programs, within DOJ, provides leadership to federal, state, local, and tribal, justice systems, by disseminating state-of-the art knowledge and practices on crime-fighting strategies across America, and providing grants for the implementation of these strategies.

[36] Three of the 41 tribes that indicated that lack of notification from state prisons was a factor that applied to them did not identify whether the lack of notification was a major challenge, a minor challenge, or not a challenge.

[37] We interviewed sex offender registry and SORNA officials in 10 states where tribes that have retained their authority are located, and the officials told us that they include convicted sex offenders who live, work, or attend school on tribal lands in the state sex offender registry.

[38] 42 U.S.C. §§ 16911(10)(H), 16913(b), 16917(a), 16921(b). Sex offenders who are not sentenced to a term of imprisonment are to register not later than 3 business days after being sentenced. 42 U.S.C. §16913(b)(2). In addition, the SMART Office has interpreted the requirement to forward sex offenders' registration information "immediately" to mean within 3 business days. See 73 Fed. Reg. 38,030, 38,044, 38,060.

[39] See 42 U.S.C. §§ 16913, 16921. Under SORNA, for ineligible and delegated tribes, such notification would go to the jurisdiction carrying out the tribes' SORNA functions. We will discuss the notification requirements pertaining to these tribes later in this report. Regarding tribes that retained SORNA implementation authority as well as ineligible, and delegated tribes, notification would also go to the law enforcement agencies, schools, and public housing agencies located on the tribes' land. 42 U.S.C. § 16921(b)(2).

[40] Even though notification to tribes is a SORNA requirement, as we reported in February 2013, some states have had to amend existing state laws or enact new laws in order to implement certain SORNA provisions. See GAO-13-211. We contacted officials in 25 states to determine whether these states require their state departments of corrections or appropriate registration officials to notify tribes that have retained their authority to implement SORNA, prior to releasing a sex offender who plans to live, work, or attend school on tribal lands. These 25 states included (1) states where tribes that responded to our survey identified as having not been notified about registered sex offenders who indicated that they would be living, working, or attending school on tribal lands upon release from prison; (2) states that have substantially implemented SORNA and also have tribes that have retained their authority to implement SORNA within their borders; and (3) states whose officials we contacted previously to conduct other audit work. Officials from 20 of the 25 states responded to our requests for information.

[41] Pursuant to 18 U.S.C. § 4042, notice shall be provided to state, tribal, and local jurisdictions where one who is required to register under SORNA, is released from prison or sentenced to probation. Federal Bureau of Prisons (BOP) officials reported that the agency implemented a new policy in May 2014 to ensure the agency complies with the statutory requirements regarding notification of sex offenders' release. According to BOP officials, the new policy requires that federal correctional facilities are to mail and fax or e- mail copies of the Prisoner Release Notification form (BP-A0710) to the chief law enforcement officer and sex offender registration official(s) of the tribe when releasing a prisoner convicted of a sex offense. Federal correctional facilities are also to provide this information to the SORNA contact in the state where the tribe has territory, local law enforcement officials who are in proximity to the tribe, as well as federal probation officials in the state.

[42] To assist jurisdictions to develop, organize, and submit their substantial implementation package materials, the SMART Office developed the SORNA Substantial Implementation Checklist tool. To complete the checklist, states must identify the specific statute or regulation that is to fulfill each SORNA requirement, including forwarding sex offender information to other relevant SORNA jurisdictions. The SMART Office also requires that states that have a tribe or tribes eligible to implement SORNA located within their boundaries provide MOAs or other information-sharing agreements to facilitate notification of sex offender release. For states that have substantially implemented SORNA, the SMART Office uses this information as the basis for an additional section titled "Tribal Considerations" in these states' Substantial Implementation Review reports.

[43] Tribes may have MOAs with local law enforcement officials who authorize these officials to carry out certain law enforcement functions on tribal lands.

[44] The Byrne Justice Memorial Discretionary Grants Program is a key provider of federal criminal justice funding to state and local jurisdictions. Established to streamline justice funding and grant administration, the Byrne JAG Program allows states, tribes, and local governments to support a broad range of activities to prevent and control crime based on their own local needs and conditions. See 42 U.S.C. §§ 3750-3758. The Adam Walsh Act Implementation Grant Program assists jurisdictions eligible to implement SORNA with developing or enhancing programs designed to implement the law. See 42 U.S.C. §§ 16925(c), 16945(c)(2).

[45] Federal, state, tribal, and local law enforcement agencies conduct compliance operations to ensure sex offenders within a certain area reside at their registered address or are otherwise compliant with sex offender registration laws.

[46] 25 U.S.C. § 2802(c)(1).

[47] 25 U.S.C. § 2802(c)(9), (12).

[48] Tribes with self-governance compacts operate their tribal law enforcement agencies themselves, tribes with self-determination contracts perform criminal investigation and police services under BIA oversight, and direct service tribes receive all law enforcement services directly from BIA. In some cases, the tribe provides uniformed police services and BIA continues to provide criminal investigation services. According to BIA, SORNA-related functions, such as arresting sex offenders who fail to comply with registration requirements, are the responsibility of uniformed police rather than criminal investigators.

[49] The BIA OJS senior official did not recall when the SMART Office provided BIA with the initial list of tribes that had retained their SORNA implementation authority.

[50] The types of additional assistance these tribes indicated they would like from BIA include funding, equipment, or the manpower to perform at least some aspects of their sex offender registry programs.

[51] 42 U.S.C. § 16927; 73 Fed. Reg. at 38,039.

[52] According to GAO's analysis of data from the SMART Office, there are 15 states with delegated tribes; however, officials from only 13 states responded to our inquiry, including 1 official who incorrectly reported that the state had not been delegated authority for any tribe and had no delegated tribes. Therefore, we received valid responses from only 12 states.

[53] 42 U.S.C. § 16921(b). The SORNA National Guidelines interpret "immediately" as within 3 business days. See 73 Fed. Reg. at 38,060.

[54] We obtained data from the Department of Education specifically regarding only public schools located on tribal lands, therefore, there may be additional tribes that have private schools on their lands; however, we did not obtain this information.

[55] See 73 Fed. Reg. at 38,061.

[56] 42 U.S.C. §§ 16911(1)-(3), 16918(c)(1).

[57] At the time of our survey, 166 tribes had retained their authority to implement SORNA. We did not survey 4 of the 166 because, according to the SMART Office, these tribes are either newly recognized tribes that have not elected whether or not to implement SORNA, or are still in the process of acquiring land. These tribes include the Cayuga Nation, the Delaware Tribe of Indians, the Samish Indian Nation, and the Shinnecock Indian Nation. We did not also survey the Onondaga Indian Nation because tribal officials told us at the time of our survey that they were in the process of delegating their SORNA authority to the state and had not taken any actions to implement the act.

[58] An electronic supplement to this report provides the survey results. See GAO, *Sex Offender Registration and Notification Act,: Survey of Federally Recognized Tribes on Implementation of the Act* (GAO-15-30SP, November 2014), an E-supplement to GAO-15-23, (Washington, D.C.: Oct. 16, 2014).

[59] The Bureau of Indian Affairs provides direct services, such as law enforcement services, to certain tribes, commonly referred to as direct service tribes, that do not operate certain programs themselves. 25 U.S.C. §§ 450f, 2802(c)(1).

[60] NCIC is a computerized index of criminal justice information (i.e., criminal record history information, fugitives, stolen properties, and missing persons) that is available to authorized federal, state, and local law enforcement and other criminal justice agencies 24 hours a day, throughout the year. NSOR is a national database within the FBI's NCIC that authorized federal, state, local, territorial, and tribal law enforcement officials can use to gain access to information on registered sex offenders throughout the United States.

[61] SORNA required eligible tribes wishing to implement the act to submit a resolution within a year of the act's enactment, electing to implement the law themselves as opposed to delegating their authority to implement to a state. 42 U.S.C. § 16927(a).

In: Sex Offender Registration within Indian Tribes ISBN: 978-1-63482-400-2
Editor: Angelica K. Bishop

Chapter 2

FAILURE TO REGISTER AS A SEX OFFENDER: A LEGAL ANALYSIS OF 18 U.S.C. 2250*

Charles Doyle

SUMMARY

Section 2250 outlaws an individual's failure to comply with federal Sex Offender Registration and Notification Act (SORNA) requirements. SORNA demands that an individual—previously convicted of a qualifying federal, state, or foreign sex offense—register with state, territorial, or tribal authorities. Individuals must register in every jurisdiction in which they live, work, or attend school. They must also update the information whenever they move, or change their employment or educational status. Section 2250 applies only under one of several jurisdictional circumstances: the individual was previously convicted of a qualifying federal sex offense; the individual travels in interstate or foreign commerce; or the individual enters, leaves, or resides in Indian country.

Individuals charged with a violation of §2250 may be subject to preventive detention or to a series of pre-trial release conditions. If convicted, they face imprisonment for not more than 10 years and/or a fine of not more

* This is an edited, reformatted and augmented version of a Congressional Research Service publication, CRS Report for Congress R42692, dated July 25, 2013.

than $250,000 as well as the prospect of a post-imprisonment term of supervised release of not less than 5 years. An offender guilty of a §2250 offense, who also commits a federal crime of violence, is subject to an additional penalty of imprisonment for up to 30 years and not less than 5 years for the violent crime.

The Attorney General has exercised his statutory authority to make SORNA applicable to qualifying convictions occurring prior to its enactment. The Supreme Court rejected the suggestion of the United States Court of Appeals for the Fifth Circuit that Congress lacks the constitutional authority to make §2250 applicable, on the basis of a prior federal offense and intrastate noncompliance, to individuals who had served their sentence and been released from federal supervision prior to SORNA's enactment, *United States v. Kebodeaux*, 134 S.Ct. 2496 (2013).

The Fifth Circuit's *Kebodeaux* opinion aside, the lower federal appellate courts have almost uniformly rejected challenges to §2250's constitutional validity. Those challenges have included arguments under the Constitution's Ex Post Facto, Due Process, Cruel and Unusual Punishment, Commerce, Necessary and Proper, and Spending Clauses.

INTRODUCTION

Federal law punishes convicted sex offenders for failure to register under the Sex Offender Registration and Notification Act (SORNA), 18 U.S.C. 2250. The offense consists of three elements: (1) an obligation to register with the authorities in any jurisdiction in which the individual lives, works, or attends school; (2) the knowing failure to comply with registration requirements; and (3) a jurisdictional element, i.e., (a) an obligation to register as a consequence of a prior qualifying federal conviction or (b)(i) travel in interstate or foreign commerce, (ii) travel into or out of Indian country; or (iii) residence in Indian country.[1] Violators face imprisonment for not more than 10 years. If an offender also commits a federal crime of violence, he is subject to an additional penalty for that offense of imprisonment for not more than 30 years, but not less than 5 years.[2]

Background

SORNA is a product of the Adam Walsh Child Protection and Safety Act.[3] It calls for a revision of an earlier nation-wide sex offender registration system. Its predecessor, the Jacob Wetterling Act, encouraged the states to establish and maintain a registration system.[4] Each of them had done so.[5] Their efforts, however, though often consistent, were hardly uniform.[6]

The Walsh Act preserves the basic structure of the Wetterling Act, expands upon it, and makes more specific matters that were previously left to individual state choice. The Walsh Act contemplates a nationwide, state-based, publicly available, contemporaneously accurate, online system. [7] Jurisdictions that fail to meet the Walsh Act's threshold requirements face the loss of a portion of their federal criminal justice assistance grants.[8]

The Walsh Act vested the Attorney General with authority to determine the extent to which SORNA would apply to those with qualifying convictions committed prior to enactment.[9] He has promulgated implementing regulations imposing the registration requirements on those with pre-enactment convictions.[10]

Conscious of the legal and technical adjustments required of the states, the Walsh Act afforded jurisdictions an extension to make the initial modifications necessary to bring their systems into compliance.[11] Thereafter, states not yet in compliance have been allowed to use the penalty portion of their federal justice assistance funds for that purpose.[12] The Justice Department indicates that 15 states are now in substantial compliance with the 2006 legislation.[13]

Elements

Section 2250 convictions require the government to prove that (1) the defendant had an obligation under SORNA to register and to maintain the currency of his registration information; (2) that the defendant knowingly failed to comply; and (3) that one of the section's jurisdictional prerequisites has been satisfied.[14]

Obligation to Register and Maintain Registration

Registration Requirements

SORNA directs anyone previously convicted of a federal, state, local, tribal, or foreign qualifying offense to register and to keep his registration information current in each jurisdiction in which he resides, or is an employee or student.[15] SORNA defines broadly the terms "student," "employee," and "resides," so that for example, the term "employee encompasses those who are self-employed and those who are not compensated."[16] Registrants who relocate or who change their names, jobs, or schools have three days to appear and update their registration.[17] The courts have said that the obligation runs from the time of departure rather than arrival, that is, from when the offender leaves his former residence, job, or school rather than when he acquires a new residence or a new job or enrolls in a different school.[18]

Qualifying Convictions

Only those who have been convicted of a qualifying sex offense need register. There are five classes of qualifying offenses: (1) designated federal sex offenses; (2) specified military offenses; (3) crimes identified as one of the "special offenses against a minor"; (4) crimes in which some sexual act or sexual conduct is an element; and (5) attempts or conspiracies to commit any offense in one of these other classes of qualifying offenses.[19]

Federal Qualifying Offenses

"A Federal offense (including an offense prosecuted under section 1152 or 1153 of title 18) under section 1591, or chapter 109A, 110 (other than section 2257, 2257A, or 2258), or 117, of title 18:"[20]

- 18 U.S.C. 1591 (sex trafficking of children or by force or fraud)
- 18 U.S.C. 2241 (aggravated sexual abuse)
- 18 U.S.C. 2242 (sexual abuse)
- 18 U.S.C. 2243 (sexual abuse of ward or child)
- 18 U.S.C. 2244 (abusive sexual contact)
- 18 U.S.C. 2245 (sexual abuse resulting in death)
- 18 U.S.C. 2251 (sexual exploitation of children)
- 18 U.S.C. 2251A (selling or buying children)
- 18 U.S.C. 2252 (transporting, distributing or selling child sexually exploitive material)
- 18 U.S.C. 2252A (transporting or distributing child pornography)

- 18 U.S.C. 2252B (misleading Internet domain names)
- 18 U.S.C. 2252C (misleading Internet website source codes)
- 18 U.S.C. 2260 (making child sexually exploitative material overseas for export to the U.S.)
- 18 U.S.C. 2421 (transportation of illicit sexual purposes)
- 18 U.S.C. 2422 (coercing or enticing travel for illicit sexual purposes)
- 18 U.S.C. 2423 (travel involving illicit sexual activity with a child)
- 18 U.S.C. 2424 (filing false statement concerning an alien for illicit sexual purposes)
- 18 U.S.C. 2425 (interstate transmission of information about a child relating to illicit sexual activity).

Military Qualifying Offenses

- UCMJ art. 120: Rape and Carnal Knowledge
- UCMJ art. 125: Forcible Sodomy and Sodomy of a Minor
- UCMJ art. 133: Conduct Unbecoming an Officer (involving any sexually violent offense or a criminal offense of a sexual nature against a Minor or kidnapping of a Minor)
- UCMJ art. 134: General Article involving:
    - prostitution of a minor;
    - indecent assault;
    - assault with intent to commit rape;
    - assault with intent to commit sodomy;
    - indecent act with a minor;
    - indecent language to a minor;
    - kidnapping of a minor (by a person not parent);
    - pornography involving a minor;
    - conduct prejudicial to good order and discipline (involving any sexually violent offense or a criminal offense of a sexual nature against a minor or kidnapping of a minor);
    - assimilative crime conviction (of a sexually violent offense or a criminal offense of a sexual nature against a minor or kidnapping of a minor);
- UCMJ art. 80: Attempt (to commit any of the foregoing)
- UCMJ art. 81: Conspiracy (to commit any of the foregoing)
- UCMJ art. 82: Solicitation (to commit any of the foregoing).[21]

Specified Offenses against a Child under 18

Federal, state, local, tribal, military, or foreign offenses involving:

- An offense (unless committed by a parent or guardian) involving kidnapping.
- An offense (unless committed by a parent or guardian) involving false imprisonment.
- Solicitation to engage in sexual conduct.
- Use in a sexual performance.
- Solicitation to practice prostitution.
- Video voyeurism as described in section 1801 of title 18.
- Possession, production, or distribution of child pornography.
- Criminal sexual conduct involving a minor, or the use of the Internet to facilitate or attempt such conduct.
- Any conduct that by its nature is a sex offense against a minor.[22]

Crimes with a Sex Element

Any federal, state, local, military, or foreign "criminal offense that has an element involving a sexual act or sexual contact with another."[23]

Attempt or Conspiracy

Any attempt or conspiracy to commit one of the other qualifying offenses.[24]

Juvenile Adjudications and Foreign Convictions

Juvenile adjudications involving qualifying offenses trigger SORNA's reporting requirements only (1) if the individual was 14 years of age or older at the time of the misconduct that gave rise to the finding and (2) the misconduct was comparable to or more severe than aggravated sexual abuse (as defined in 18 U.S.C. 2241) or was an attempt or conspiracy to engage in such misconduct. Aggravated sexual abuse extends to sexual acts committed by force, threat, or incapacitating the victim.[25] The Federal Juvenile Delinquency Act limits disclosure of federal judicial delinquency proceedings.[26] It does not, however, excuse compliance with SORNA's registration requirements.[27]

SORNA only insists upon coverage of those foreign convictions "obtained with sufficient safeguards for fundamental fairness and due process of the accused." The *National Guidelines* state that "[s]ex offense convictions under the laws of any foreign country are deemed to have been obtained with sufficient safeguards for fundamental fairness and due process if the U.S. State Department, in its Country Reports on Human Rights Practices, has concluded that an independent judiciary generally (or vigorously) enforced the right to a fair trial in that country during the year in which the conviction occurred."[28] They go on to point out, however, that SORNA establishes only minimum requirements. States and other jurisdictions remain free to require registration based on any foreign conviction.[29]

Pre-SORNA Convictions

SORNA's registration requirement is time neutral. It simply states that sex offenders must register.[30] It goes on to say, however, that the "Attorney General shall have the authority to specify the applicability of the requirements of [SORNA] to sex offenders convicted before [its] enactment."[31] The Supreme Court resolved a split among the lower federal courts when it declared in *Reynolds v. United States* that SORNA's "registration requirements do not apply to pre-Act offenders until the Attorney General specifies that they do apply."[32]

Yet, the Court left unresolved the question of when the Attorney General had specified that they apply. This too is a matter upon which the lower federal appellate courts disagree. The issue involves Administrative Procedure Act compliance. The Administrative Procedure Act (APA) provides that, as a general rule, the public must be given an opportunity to comment before a regulatory proposal becomes final.[33] Good cause may excuse the need to honor this "notice and comment" prerequisite.[34]

The Attorney General issued an Interim Rule on February 28, 2007, in which he announced that SORNA's requirements "apply to all sex offenders, including sex offenders convicted of the offense for which registration is required prior the enactment of that Act."[35] He claimed, as good cause to dispense with notice and comment, the need to eliminate uncertainty and "to protect the public from sex offenders who failed to register."[36]

On July 2, 2008, after a notice and comment period, the Attorney General promulgated the *National Guidelines*, which cited the Interim Rule for the proposition that SORNA's date of enactment (July 27, 2006) marked the date upon which all sex offenders, including those whose convictions predated SORNA, were bound by its dictates.[37] On December 29, 2010, the Attorney General promulgated a final rule, effective January 28, 2011, that declared the 2007 Interim Rule final with respect to SORNA's application to convictions that predate its enactment.[38]

Three circuits rejected the argument that APA noncompliance invalidated the Attorney General's effort in the 2007 Interim Rule to bring pre-enactment convictions within SORNA requirements.[39] Four others found the Attorney General had failed to meet APA standards.[40] One found error and that the government had not shown that the error was prejudicial as it was required to do.[41] Another found the error harmless.[42] The other pair concluded that the procedures used to promulgate the 2008 *National Guidelines* satisfied APA requirements.[43] In the view of these last two circuits, SORNA application to pre-enactment convictions became effective on August 1, 2008, the 30 days after valid promulgation required by the APA.[44] Whichever view the other circuits find most convincing, they are likely to settle on an application date no later than August 1, 2008.

Knowing Failure to Register

Section 2250's second element is a knowing failure to register or to maintain current registration information as required by SORNA. The government must show that the defendant knew of his obligation and failed to honor it; the prosecution need not show that he knew he was bound to do so by federal law generally or by SORNA specifically.[45]

Jurisdictional Elements

Section 2250 permits conviction on the basis of any three jurisdictional elements: a prior conviction of one of the federal qualifying offenses; residence in, or travel to or from, Indian country; or travel in interstate or foreign commerce.

Federal Crimes

Interstate travel is not required for a conviction under §2250. An individual need only have a knowing failure to register and a prior conviction for a qualifying sex offense under federal law or the law of the District of Columbia, the Code of Military Justice, tribal law, or the law of a United States territory or possession.[46] Federal jurisdiction flows from the jurisdictional basis for the underlying qualifying offense.[47]

Indian Country

Travel to or from Indian country, or living there, will also satisfy §2250's jurisdictional requirement. "Indian country" consists primarily of Indian reservations, lands over which the United States enjoys state-like exclusive or concurrent legislative jurisdiction.[48]

Travel

Interstate travel is the most commonly invoked of §2250's jurisdictional elements. It applies simply to anyone who travels in interstate or foreign commerce with a prior federal or state qualifying offense who fails to register or maintain his registration. The qualifying offense may predate SORNA's enactment; the travel may not. Section "2250 does not extend to pre-enactment travel."[49]

Affirmative Defense

The Walsh Act imposes the obligation to register with state authorities on convicted sex offenders, even when state law does not require registration.[50] Prior to the Walsh Act, more than a few state sex offender registration laws applied only to convictions occurring subsequent to their enactment or only to a narrower range of offenses than contemplated in the Walsh Act. As a consequence of the Walsh Act and the Attorney General's determination, states must often adjust their registration laws in order to come into compliance. Conscious of the delays that might attend this process, §2250(b) affords offenders an affirmative defense when they seek to register with state authorities, are turned away, and remain persistent in their efforts to register: "In a prosecution for a violation under subsection (a), it is an affirmative defense that - (1) uncontrollable circumstances prevented the individual from complying; (2) the individual did not contribute to the creation of such circumstances in reckless disregard of the requirement to comply; and (3) the individual complied as soon as such circumstances ceased to exist."[51]

Consequences

Federal bail laws permit the prosecution to request a pre-trial detention hearing prior to the pre-trial release of anyone charged with a violation of §2250.[52] The individual may only be released prior to trial under condition, among others, that he be electronically monitored; be subject to restrictions on his personal associations, residence, or travel; report regularly to authorities; and be subject to a curfew.[53]

Upon conviction, the individual may be sentenced to imprisonment for a term of not more than 10 years and/or fined not more than $250,000.[54] Section 2250 also sets a penalty of not more than 30 years, but not less than 5 years, in prison for the commission of a federal crime of violence when the offender has also violated §2250.[55] In any event, those sentenced to imprisonment are also sentenced to a term of supervised release of not less than 5 years, rather than a term of not more than 5 years that attends the more serious federal felonies.[56]

CONSTITUTIONAL CONSIDERATIONS

Much of the early litigation relating to §2250 involves constitutional challenges involving either the section or SORNA. The attacks take one of two forms. One argues that SORNA or §2250 operates in a manner which the Constitution specifically forbids, for example in its clauses on Ex Post Facto laws, Due Process, and Cruel and Unusual Punishment. The other argues that the Constitution does not grant Congress the legislative authority to enact either §2250 or SORNA. These challenges probe the boundaries of the Commerce Clause, the Necessary and Proper Clause, and the Spending Clause, among others.

The Supreme Court addressed two of the most common constitutional issues associated with sex offender registration before the enactment of SORNA. One involved Ex Post Facto, *Smith v. Doe*;[57] the other Due Process, *Connecticut Department of Public Safety v. Doe*.[58]

Ex Post Facto

Neither the states nor the federal government may enact laws which operate Ex Post Facto.[59] The prohibition covers both statutes that outlaw conduct which was innocent when it occurred and statutes that authorize imposition of a greater penalty for a crime than applied when the crime occurred.[60] The prohibitions, however, apply only to criminal statutes or to civil statutes whose intent or effect is so punitive as to belie any but a penal characterization.[61]

In *Smith*, the Supreme Court dealt with the Ex Post Facto issue in the context of the Alaska sex offender registration statute. It found the statute civil, not punitive, and consequently its retroactive application did not violate the Ex Post Facto Clause.[62] Its analysis[63] has colored the lower federal courts' treatment of Ex Post Facto challenges to §2250 and SORNA. "Relying on *Smith*, circuit courts have consistently held that SORNA does not violate the Ex Post Facto Clause,"[64] with one apparently limited exception. The Ninth Circuit initially held that the SORNA obligations for pre-enactment juveniles constituted punishment, because they stripped juveniles of the confidentiality that then surrounded juvenile proceedings.[65] Thus, their enforcement against such juveniles would constitute an Ex Post Facto violation, the Ninth Circuit decided.[66] It subsequently concluded that "not all applications of SORNA to individuals based on juvenile sex offender determinations are sufficiently punitive to violate the Ex Post Facto Clause."[67] This is particular true, the Circuit opined, when SORNA did not result in a loss of confidentiality because of the disclosure requirements that accompanied the original qualifying juvenile adjudication.[68]

Due Process

The Supreme Court's assessment of state sex offender registration statutes has been less dispositive of process issues due to the variety of challenges brought. Neither the federal nor state governments may deny a person of "life, liberty, or property, without due process of law."[69] Due process requirements take many forms. They may not punish without notice: "[a] conviction fails to comport with due process if the statute under which it is obtained fails to provide a person of ordinary intelligence fair notice of what is prohibited, or is so standardless that it authorizes or encourages seriously discriminatory enforcement."[70] They may not restrain liberty or the enjoyment of property without an opportunity to be heard: "[a]n essential principle of due process is that a deprivation of life, liberty, or property be preceded by notice and opportunity for hearing appropriate to the nature of the case."[71] They may not impose punishment or restrictions that are so fundamentally unfair as to constitute a violation of substantive due process.

In *Connecticut Dept. of Public Safety v. Doe*, the Court found no due process infirmity in the Connecticut sex offender registration regime in spite of its failure to afford offenders an opportunity to prove they were not dangerous.[72] Doe suffered no injury from the absence of a pre-registration hearing to determine his dangerousness, in the eyes of the Court, because the system required registration of all sex offenders, both those who were dangerous and those who were not.[73] *Connecticut Dept. of Public Safety* forecloses the assertion that offenders are entitled to a pre-registration "dangerousness" hearing; the relevant question under SORNA is prior conviction not dangerousness.[74]

In *Lambert v. California*, the Court dealt with the issue of sufficiency of notice. There, the Court held invalid a city ordinance that required all felony offenders to register within five days of their arrival in the city.[75] The Court explained that "[w]here a person did not know of the duty to register and where there was no proof of the probability of such knowledge, he may not be convicted consistently with due process."[76] Since "by the time that Congress enacted SORNA, every state had a sex offender registration law in place,"[77] attempts to build on *Lambert* have been rejected, because the courts concluded that offenders knew or should have known of their duty to register.[78] Suggestions that differences between state and federal requirements result in impermissible vagueness have fared no better.[79]

To qualify as a violation of substantive due process, a governmental regime must intrude upon a right "deeply rooted in our history and traditions," or "fundamental to our concept of constitutionally ordered liberty."[80] Perhaps because the threshold is so high, §2250 and SORNA have only infrequently been questioned on substantive due process grounds.[81]

Right to Travel

"The 'right to travel' ... embraces at least three different components. It protects the right of a citizen of one State to enter and to leave another State, the right to be treated as a welcome visitor rather than an unfriendly alien when temporarily present in the second State, and, for those travelers who elect to become permanent residents, the right to be treated like other citizens of that State."[82]

Section 2250, it has been contended, violates the right to travel because it punishes those who travel from one state to another yet fail to register, but not those who fail to register without leaving the state. The courts have responded, however, that the right must yield to compelling state interest in the prevention of future sex offenses.[83]

Cruel and Unusual Punishment

The Eighth Amendment bars the federal government from inflicting "cruel and unusual punishment."[84] A punishment is cruel and unusual within the meaning of the Eighth Amendment when it is grossly disproportionate to the offense.[85] The courts have refused to say that sentences within §2250's 10-year maximum are grossly disproportionate to the crime of failing to maintain current and accurate sex offender registration information.[86] They have also declined to hold that SORNA's registration regime itself violates the Eighth Amendment, either because they do not consider the requirements punitive or because they do not consider them grossly disproportionate.[87]

Legislative Authority

The most frequent constitutional challenge raised against SORNA and §2250 is that Congress lacked the constitutional authority to enact them. Some of these challenges speak to the breadth of Congress's constitutional powers, such as those vested under the Tax and Spend Clause, the Commerce Clause, or the Necessary and Proper Clause. Others address contextual limitations on the exercise of those of those powers imposed by such things as the non-delegation doctrine or the principles of separation of powers.

Tenth Amendment

Congress enjoys only such legislative authority as may be traced to the Constitution; the Tenth Amendment reserves to the states and the people powers not vested in it.[88] Challengers of Congress's legislative authority to enact SORNA or the Justice Department's authority to prosecute failure to comply with its demands have had to face three substantial obstacles. First, several of Congress's constitutional powers are far reaching. Among them are the powers to regulate interstate and foreign commerce, to tax and spend for the general welfare, and to enact laws necessary and proper to effectuate the authority the Constitution provides.[89] Second, although a particular statute may constitute the proper exercise of more than one constitutional power, only one is necessary for constitutional purposes.[90] Finally, until recently some courts held that the individual defendants had no standing to contest the statutory validity on the basis of constitutional provisions such as the separation of powers doctrine and the Tenth Amendment that were designed to protect the institutional interests of governmental entities rather than to protect private interests.

Standing

Several earlier courts rejected SORNA challenges under the Tenth Amendment on the grounds that the defendants had no standing. Standing refers to the question of whether a party in litigation is asserting or "standing" on his or her own rights or only upon those of another. At one time, there was no consensus among the lower federal appellate courts over whether individuals had standing to present Tenth Amendment claims.[91] More specifically, at least two circuits had held that defendants convicted under §2250 had no standing to challenge their convictions on Tenth Amendment grounds.[92]

Those courts, however, did not have the benefit of the Supreme Court's *Bond* and *Reynolds* decisions. In *Bond*, the Court pointed out that a defendant who challenges the Tenth Amendment validity of the statute under which she was convicted "seeks to vindicate her own constitutional rights.... The individual, in a proper case, can assert injury from governmental action taken in excess of the authority that federalism defines. Her rights in this regard do not belong to the state."[93] In *Reynolds*, the Court implicitly recognized the defendant's standing when at his behest it held that SORNA did not apply to pre-enactment convictions until after the Attorney General had exercised his delegated authority.[94] Yet, the fact a defendant's Tenth Amendment challenge may be heard does not mean it will succeed. Most have not succeeded.

Spending for the General Welfare

"The Congress shall have Power To lay and collect Taxes ... to pay the Debts and provide for the common Defence and general Welfare of the United States.... "[95] "Objectives not thought to be within Article I's enumerated legislative fields, may nevertheless be attained through the use of the spending power and the conditional grant of federal funds."[96] In the past, the Supreme Court has described the limits on Congress in very general terms:

> [First,] [T]he exercise of the spending power must be in pursuit of the general welfare.... Second, ... if Congress desires to condition the States' receipt of federal funds, it must do so unambiguously ... Third, ... conditions on federal grants ... [must be] []related to the federal interest in particular national projects or programs.... Finally, ... other constitutional provisions may provide an independent bar to the conditional grant of federal funds.[97]

Moreover, at the end of its 2011 term in *National Federation of Business v. Sebelius*, seven Members of a highly divided Court concluded that the power of the Spending Clause may not be exercised to coerce state participation in a federal program.[98] Congress may use the spending power to induce state participation; it may not present the choice under such circumstances that a state has no realistic alternative but to acquiesce.[99]

SORNA establishes minimum standards for the state sex offender registers and authorizes the Attorney General to enforce compliance by reducing by up to 10% the funds a non-complying state would receive in criminal justice assistance funds.[100] Some defendants have suggested that this impermissibly commandeers state officials to administer a federal program and therefore exceeds Congress's authority under the Spending Clause. As a general matter, while Congress may encourage state participation in a federal program, it is not constitutionally free to require state legislators or executive officials to act to enforce or administer a federal regulatory program.[101] To date, the federal appellate courts have held that SORNA's reduction in federal law enforcement assistance grants for a state's failure to comply falls on the encouragement rather than directive side of the constitutional line.[102] The fact that most states do not feel compelled to bring their systems into full SORNA compliance may lend credence to that assessment.[103]

Commerce Clause

"The Congress shall have Power ... To regulate Commerce with foreign Nations, and among the several States, and with the Indian Tribes."[104] The Supreme Court explained in *Lopez* and again in *Morrison* that Congress's Commerce Clause power is broad but not boundless.

> Modern Commerce Clause jurisprudence has identified three broad categories of activity that Congress may regulate under its commerce power. First, Congress may regulate the use of the channels of interstate commerce. Second, Congress is empowered to regulate and protect the instrumentalities of interstate commerce, or persons or things in interstate commerce, even though the threat may come only from intrastate activities. Finally, Congress' commerce authority includes the power to regulate those activities having a substantial relation to interstate commerce ... i.e., those activities that substantially affect interstate commerce.[105]

The lower federal appellate courts have rejected Commerce Clause attacks on §2250 in the interstate travel cases, because there they believe §2250 "fits comfortably with the first two *Lopez* prongs[, i.e. the regulation of (1) the "channels" of interstate commerce and (2) the "instrumentalities" of interstate commerce]."[106] They have rejected Commerce Clause attacks on SORNA ("§16913 [SORNA] is an unconstitutional exercise of Congress's Commerce Clause power and because lack of compliance with §16913 is a necessary element of §2250, §2250 is also unconstitutional") based on the Necessary and Proper Clause:

> Requiring sex offenders to update their registrations due to intrastate changes of address or employment status is a perfectly logical way to help ensure that states will more effectively be able to track sex offenders when they do cross state lines. To the extent that §16913 regulates solely intrastate activity, its means are reasonably adapted to the attainment of a legitimate end under the commerce power and therefore proper.[107]

Necessary and Proper

The Supreme Court in *Comstock* described the breadth of Congress's authority under the Necessary and Proper Clause in the context of another Walsh Act provision. The Walsh Act authorizes the Attorney General to hold federal inmates beyond their release date in order to initiate federal civil commitment proceedings for the sexually dangerous.[108] Comstock and others questioned application of the statute on the grounds that it exceeded Congress's legislative authority under the Commerce and Necessary and Proper Clauses.[109]

The Court pointed out that the Necessary and Proper Clause has long been understood to empower Congress to enact legislation "rationally related to the implementation of a constitutionally enumerated power."[110] Moreover, be the chain clear and unbroken, the challenged statute need not necessarily be directly linked to a constitutionally enumerated power.[111] The *Comstock* "statute is a 'necessary and proper' means of exercising the federal authority that permits Congress to create federal criminal laws [(to carry into effect its Commerce Clause power for instance)], to punish their violation, to imprison violators, to provide appropriately for those imprisoned, and to maintain the security of those who are not imprisoned but who may be affected by the federal imprisonment of others."[112]

The Court, however, warned that its conclusion was predicated on several factors specific to the case before it.[113] Acting on this suggestion, the Fifth Circuit, sitting en banc, erroneously concluded that SORNA, as applied to Kebodeaux, rested beyond Congress's legislative reach.[114]

Kebodeaux had been convicted by a military court for having sexual relations with a consenting fifteen year old while he was a twenty-one year old airman. He was sentenced to six months and given a bad conduct discharge in 1999. He registered as a sex offender with Texas authorities in 2007. He was convicted for violating §2250 in 2008, after he failed to report that he had relocated from El Paso to San Antonio.[115]

The Constitution empowers Congress to make rules for the governing and regulation of the armed forces.[116] It also vests Congress with broad implementing authority to enact legislation necessary and proper to carry into effect this military governance power and the other powers conveyed by the Constitution.[117] The Fifth Circuit believed that, unlike the *Comstock* statute, the application of SORNA was not closely proximate to a federal custodial interest and was sweeping in its conceptual foundation ("[t]hat reasoning opens the door ... to congressional power over anyone who was ever convicted of a federal crime of any sort").[118]

Justice Breyer, the author of the Supreme Court's majority opinion, however, concluded that the Fifth Circuit had overlooked an easily missed bridge between the military governance power and the SORNA implementation of that power.[119] At the time of his conviction and subsequent release, a federal predecessor, the Wetterling Act, required Kebodeaux to register with Texas state authorities and made his failure to do so a federal crime.[120] Much like *Comstock* , the Wetterling Act addressed the consequences of the release of sex offenders from the federal custody. Thus, Congress might validly elect in the Wetterling Act to implement its military governance authority by fixing the consequences of federal prisoners discharged from federal custody following a court martial.[121] By the same token, it might validly modify and expand in SORNA the consequences established in the Wetterling Act.[122]

Separation of Powers: Non-Delegation

The first section of the first article of the Constitution declares that "[a]ll legislative Powers herein granted shall be vested in Congress of the United States.... "[123] This means that "Congress manifestly is not permitted to abdicate or to transfer to others the essential legislative functions with which it is [constitutionally] vested."[124] This non-delegation doctrine, however, does not prevent Congress from delegating the task of filling in the details of its legislative handiwork, as long as it provides "intelligent principles" to direct the effectuation of its legislative will.[125] The circuit courts have yet to be persuaded that Congress's SORNA delegation to the Attorney General violates the non-delegation doctrine.[126]

End Notes

[1] 18 U.S.C. 2250(a).
[2] 18 U.S.C. 2250(c).
[3] P.L. 109-248, 120 Stat. 587 (2006), 42 U.S.C. 16901-16945, 18 U.S.C. 2250.
[4] 42 U.S.C. 14071-14073 (repealed).
[5] Citations to the state statutes in effect at the time of the Walsh Act's enactment appear in CRS Report RL33967, *Adam Walsh Child Protection and Safety Act: A Legal Analysis*, 1-2 n.8.
[6] *Reynolds v. United States*, 132 S.Ct. 975, 978 (2012)(here and throughout internal citations have generally been omitted)("The new federal Act reflects Congress' awareness that pre-Act registration law consisted of a patchwork of federal and 50 individual state registration systems").
[7] Office of the Attorney General, *The National Guidelines for Sex Offender Registration and Notification (National Guidelines)*, 73 *Federal Register* 38030, 38044-45 (July 2, 2008).
[8] 42 U.S.C. 16925.
[9] 42 U.S.C. 16913(d).
[10] 72 *Federal Register* 8894-897 (February 28, 2007)(interim rule); 75 *Federal Register* 18849-853 (December 29, 2010)(final rule), 28 C.F.R. pt. 72.
[11] 42 U.S.C. 16924.
[12] U.S. Department of Justice, Office of Sex Offender Sentencing, Monitoring, Apprehending, Registering, and Tracking, *Requests for Reallocation of Byrne JAG Funding Penalty,* SMART Watch (Spring 2012), available at http://www.ojp.gov/smart/smarwatch/12_spring/news-1.html.
[13] United States Department of Justice, Office of Sex Offender Sentencing, Monitoring, Apprehending, Registering, and Tracking, *Jurisdictions That Have Substantially Implemented SORNA*, available at http://www.ojp.usdoj.gov/smart/newsroom_jurisdictions_sorna.htm.
[14] 18 U.S.C. 2250(a)("Whoever - (1) is required to register under the Sex Offender Registration and Notification Act; (2)(A) is a sex offender as defined for the purposes of the Sex Offender Registration and Notification Act by reason of a conviction under Federal law (including the Uniform Code of Military Justice), the law of the District of Columbia, Indian tribal law, or the law of any territory or possession of the United States; or (B) travels in interstate or foreign commerce, or enters or leaves, or resides in, Indian country; and (3) knowingly fails to register or update a registration as required by the Sex Offender Registration and Notification Act; shall be fined under this title or imprisoned not more than 10 years, or both").
[15] "A sex offender shall register, and keep the registration current, in each jurisdiction where the offender resides, where the offender is an employee, and where the offender is a student.... " 42 U.S.C. 16913(a). "The term 'sex offender' means an individual who was convicted of a sex offense," 42 U.S.C. 16911(1). "[T]he term 'sex offense' means – a criminal offense ... a [designated] Federal offense ... [or] a military offense.... " 42 U.S.C. 16911(5)(A)(1). "The term 'criminal offense' means a State, local, tribal, foreign, or military offense ... or other criminal offense," 42 U.S.C. 16911(6).
[16] 42 U.S.C. 16911(12)("The term 'employee' includes an individual who is self-employed or works for any other entity, whether compensated or not"); see also, 42 U.S.C. 16911(11)("The term 'student' means an individual who enrolls in or attends an educational institution, including (whether public or private) a secondary school, trade or professional

school, and institution of higher education"); 42 U.S.C. 16911(13) ("The term 'resides' means, with respect to an individual, the location of the individual's home or other place where the individual habitually lives").

[17] 42 U.S.C. 16913(c)("A sex offender shall, not later than 3 business days after each change of name, residence, employment, or student status, appear in person in at least 1 jurisdiction involved pursuant to subsection (a) and inform that jurisdiction of all changes in the information required for that offender in the sex offender registry. That jurisdiction shall immediately provide that information to all other jurisdictions in which the offender is required to register").

[18] *United States v. Murphy*, 664 F.3d 798, 800-803 (10th Cir. 2011); *United States v. Van Buren*, 599 F.3d 170, 174-75 (2d Cir. 2010); *United States v. Voice*, 622 F.3d 870, 875 (8th Cir. 2010). Each of these cases involved a change of residence rather than employment or education, but the distinction should make no difference.

[19] 42 U.S.C. 16911(1), (5), (7).

[20] 42 U.S.C. 16911(5)(A)(iii).

[21] U.S. Department of Defense, *Department of Defense Instruction 1325.7, Enclosure 27.*

[22] 42 U.S.C. 16911((7), (5)(A)(ii), (6), (14).

[23] 42 U.S.C. 16911(5)(A)(i). SORNA defines neither "sexual act" nor "sexual contact." The terms are defined elsewhere in the United States Code as follows: "(2) the term 'sexual act' means - (A) contact between the penis and the vulva or the penis and the anus, and for purposes of this subparagraph contact involving the penis occurs upon penetration, however slight; (B) contact between the mouth and the penis, the mouth and the vulva, or the mouth and the anus; (C) the penetration, however slight, of the anal or genital opening of another by a hand or finger or by any object, with an intent to abuse, humiliate, harass, degrade, or arouse or gratify the sexual desire of any person; or (D) the intentional touching, not through the clothing, of the genitalia of another person who has not attained the age of 16 years with an intent to abuse, humiliate, harass, degrade, or arouse or gratify the sexual desire of any person;"

"(3) the term 'sexual contact' means the intentional touching, either directly or through the clothing, of the genitalia, anus, groin, breast, inner thigh, or buttocks of any person with an intent to abuse, humiliate, harass, degrade, or arouse or gratify the sexual desire of any person," 18 U.S.C. 2246(2), (3), adopted by cross reference in 20 U.S.C. 6777(e)(8); 20 U.S.C. 9134(f)(7)(E); 47 U.S.C. 254(h)(7)(H); and 47 U.S.C. 902 note (P.L. 106-554, 114 Stat. 2763A-336 (2000).

[24] 42 U.S.C. 16911((a)(A)(v).

[25] 42 U.S.C. 16911(8); 18 U.S.C. 2241; cf., *National Guidelines*, 73 *Federal Register* at 38050.

[26] 18 U.S.C. 5038(a).

[27] *United States v. Under Seal*, 709 F.3d 257, 261-63 (4th Cir. 2013).

[28] *National Guidelines*, 73 *Federal Register* at 38050.

[29] *Id.* at 38051.

[30] 42 U.S.C. 16913(a)("A sex offender shall register ... ").

[31] 42 U.S.C. 16913(d).

[32] *Reynolds v. United States*, 132 S.Ct. 975, 978 (2012).

[33] 5 U.S.C. 553.

[34] 5 U.S.C. 553(b), (d).

[35] 72 *Federal Register* 8894, 8897 (February 28, 2007), 28 C.F.R. §72.3.

[36] 72 *Federal Register* 8894, 8896 (February 28, 2007), 28 C.F.R. pt.72

[37] *National Guidelines*, 73 *Federal Register* at 38046 ("Rather, SORNA's requirements took effect, when SORNA was enacted on July 26, 2007, and they have applied since that time to all sex offenders, including those whose convictions predate SORNA's enactment. See 72 FR 8894, 8895-96 (February 28, 2007)").

[38] 73 *Federal Register* 81849 (December 28, 2010).

[39] *United States v. Dean*, 604 F.3d 1275, 1278-282 (11th Cir. 2010)("The Attorney General had good cause to bypass the Administrative Procedure Act's notice and comment requirements"); *United State v. Gould*, 568 F.3d 459, 470 (4th Cir. 2009)("[T]he Attorney General had good cause to invoke the exception to providing the 30-day notice"); *United States v. Dixon*, 551 F.3d 578, 583 (7th Cir. 2008)(characterizing the APA argument as "frivolous").

[40] *United States v. Reynolds*, 710 F.3d 498, 510-14 (3d Cir. 2013); *United States v. Johnson*, 632 F.3d 912, 927-30 (5th Cir. 2011)("[W]e do not find the Attorney General's reasons for bypassing the APA's notice-and-comment and thirty day provisions persuasive"); *United States v. Valverde*, 628 F.3d 1159, 1164-168 (9th Cir. 2010); *United States v. Cain*, 583 F.3d 408, 419-24 (6th Cir. 2009).

[41] *United States v. Reynolds*, 710 F.3d at 514-24.

[42] *United States v. Johnson*, 632 F.3d at 933 ("Because the Attorney General's rulemaking process addressed the same issues raised by Johnson and because Johnson makes no showing that the outcome of the process would have been different ... had notice been at its meticulous best, we find it is clear that the Attorney General's APA violations were harmless error").

[43] *United States v. Valverde*, 628 F.3d at 1164; *United States v. Utesch*, 596 F.3d 302, 310 (6th Cir. 2010).

[44] *United States v. Valverde*, 628 F.3d at 1169; *United States v. Stevenson*, 676 F.3d 557, 562-66 (6th Cir. 2012).

[45] *United States v. Fuller*, 627 F.3d 499, 507 (2d Cir. 2010)("[E]very Circuit to have considered the matter has held that SORNA is a general intent crime ... 'There is no language requiring specific intent or a willful failure to register such that the defendant must know his failure to register violated federal law'"), quoting, *United States v. Gould*, 568 F.3d 459, 468 (4th Cir. 2004), and citing in accord, *United States v. Shenandoah*, 595 F.3d 151, 159 (3d Cir. 2010), and *United States v. Vasquez*, 611 F.3d 325, 328-29 (7th Cir. 2010); see also, *United States v. Voice*, 622 F.3d 870, 875-66 (8th Cir. 2010); *United States v. Crowder*, 656 F.3d 870, 873-76 (9th Cir. 2011).

[46] 18 U.S.C. 2250(a)(emphasis added)("Whoever ... (2)(A) is a sex offender ... by reason of a conviction under Federal law ... *or* (B) travels in interstate or foreign commerce ... "); *United States v. Kebodeaux*, 647 F.3d 137, 142 (5th Cir. 2011), vac'd for reh'g en banc, 647 F.3d 605 (5th Cir. 2011), citing, *Carr v. United States*, 130 S.Ct. 2229, 2238 (2010)("[Section] 2250(a)(2)(A) does not depend on the interstate commerce jurisdictional hook. That subsection expressly deals with person convicted under federal sex offender statutes and is conspicuously lacking the interstate travel element of §2250(a)(2)(B)").

[47] *United States v. George*, 625 F.3d 1124, 1130 (9th Cir. 2010); cf., *United States v. Kebodeaux*, 647 F.3d at 142 ("Federal sex offender statutes themselves are promulgated under various provisions of Article I [(Congress' enumerated powers)]"); *United States v. Comstock*, 130 S.Ct. 1949, 1965 (2010)("[A] statute is a 'necessary and proper' means of exercising the federal authority that permits Congress to create federal criminal laws, to punish their violation, to imprison violators, to provide appropriately for those imprisoned, and to maintain the security of those who are not imprisoned but who may be affected by the federal imprisonment of others").

[48] 18 U.S.C. 1151 ("... [T]he term 'Indian country' ... means (a) all land within the limits of any Indian reservation under the jurisdiction of the United States Government ... , (b) all dependent Indian communities within the borders of the United States whether within the original or subsequently acquired territory thereof, and whether within or without the limits of a state, and (c) all Indian allotments, the Indian titles to which have not been extinguished, including rights- of-way running through the same").

[49] *Carr v. United States*, 130 S.Ct. 2229, 2242 (2010).

[50] 42 U.S.C. 16913(a)("A sex offender shall register ... "); *United States v. Stock*, 685 F.3d 621, 626 (6th Cir. 2012)("The obligation SORNA does impose—the obligation to register—is

imposed on sex offenders, not states.... That obligation exists whether or not a state chooses to implement SORNA's requirements and whether or not a state chooses to register sex offenders at all").

[51] 18 U.S.C. 2250(b); see also, *Kennedy v. Allera*, 612 F.3d 261, 269 (4th Cir. 2010)(emphasis in the original)("Thus, while SORNA imposes a duty *on the sex offender* to register, it nowhere imposes a requirement *on the State* to accept such registration. Indeed, the criminal provisions of SORNA also recognize that a State can refuse registration in as much as they allow, as an affirmative defense to a prosecution, the claim that 'uncontrollable circumstances prevent the individual from complying'").

[52] 18 U.S.C. 3142(f)(1)(E).

[53] 18 U.S.C. 3142(c)(1)(B).

[54] 18 U.S.C. 2250(a).

[55] 18 U.S.C. 2250(c)("(1) In general. - An individual described in subsection (a) who commits a crime of violence under Federal law (including the Uniform Code of Military Justice), the law of the District of Columbia, Indian tribal law, or the law of any territory or possession of the United States shall be imprisoned for not less than 5 years and not more than 30 years. (2) Additional punishment. - The punishment provided in paragraph (1) shall be in addition and consecutive to the punishment provided for the violation described in subsection (a)").

[56] 18 U.S.C. 3583(b), (k).

[57] 538 U.S. 84 (2003).

[58] 538 U.S. 1 (2003).

[59] U.S. Const. Art. I, §10, cl. 1; Art. I, §9, cl.3.

[60] *Stogner v. California*, 539 U.S. 607, 612 (2003).

[61] *Smith v. Doe*, 538 U.S. 84, 92 (2003)("This is the first time we have considered a claim that a sex offender registration and notification law constitutes retroactive punishment forbidden by the Ex Post Facto Clause. The framework for our inquiry, however, is well established. We must ascertain whether the legislature meant the statute to establish 'civil' proceedings. If the intention of the legislature was to impose punishment, that ends the inquiry. If, however, the intention was to enact a regulatory scheme that is civil and nonpunitive, we must further examine whether the statutory scheme is so punitive either in purpose or effect as to negate the State's intention to deem it 'civil.' Because we ordinarily defer to the legislature's stated intent, only the clearest proof will suffice to override legislative intent and transform what has been denominated a civil remedy into a criminal penalty").

[62] *Id.* at 107-108.

[63] *Id.* at 97("In analyzing the effects of the Act we refer to the seven factors noted in *Kennedy v. Mendoza-Martinez*, 372 U.S. 144, 168-69 (1963), as a useful framework.... The factors most relevant to our analysis are whether, in its necessary operation, the regulatory scheme: has been regarded in our history and traditions as a punishment; imposes an affirmative disability or restraint; promotes the traditional aims of punishment; has a rational connection to a nonpunitive purpose; or is excessive with respect to this purpose").

[64] *United States v. Felts*, 674 F.3d 599, 606 (6th Cir. 2012), citing, *United States v. DiTomasso*, 621 F.3d 17, 25 (1st Cir. 2010); *United States v. Guzman*, 591 F.3d 83, 94 (2d Cir. 2010); *United States v. Shenandoah*, 595 F.3d 151, 158-59 (3d Cir. 2010); *United States v. George*, 625 F.3d 1124, 1131 (9th Cir. 2010); *United States v. Gould*, 568 F.3d 459, 466 (4th Cir. 2009); *United States v. Young*, 585 F.3d 199, 203-06 (5th Cir. 2009); *United States v. Ambert*, 561 F.3d 1202, 1207 (11th Cir. 2009); *United States v. May*, 535 F.3d 912, 919-20 (8th Cir. 2008); *United States v. Hinckley*, 550 F.3d 926, 936 (10th Cir. 2008); see also, *United States v. W.B.H.*, 664 F.3d 848, 852-60 (11th Cir. 2011); *United States v. Leach*, 639 F.3d 769, 772-73(7th Cir. 2011).

[65] *United States v. Juvenile Male*, 590 F.3d 924, 941-42 (9th Cir. 2010), vac'd as moot, 131 S.Ct. 2860 (2011).

[66] *Id.*

[67] *United States v. Elkins*, 685 F.3d 1038, 1048 (9th Cir. 2012), citing, *United States v. Juvenile Male*, 670 F.3d 999 (9th Cir. 2012).

[68] *United States v. Elkins*, 683 F.3d at1048-49.

[69] U.S. Const. Amends. V, XIV.

[70] *United States v. Williams*, 553 U.S. 285, 304 (2008).

[71] *Hamdi v. Rumsfeld*, 542 U.S. 507, 533 (2004).

[72] *Connecticut Dept. of Public Safety v. Doe*, 538 U.S. 1 (2003).

[73] *Id.* at 7-8.

[74] *United States v. Ambert*, 561 F.3d 1202, 1208 (11th Cir. 2009).

[75] *Lambert v. California*, 355 U.S. 225 (1957).

[76] *Id.* at 229-30.

[77] *United States v. DiTomasso*, 621 F.3d 17, 26 (1st Cir. 2010).

[78] *United States v. Hester*, 589 F.3d 86, 92-3 (2d Cir. 2009)("In *Lambert*, the Supreme Court stated: 'Registration laws are common and their range is wide.... But the present ordinance is entirely different. Violation of its provisions is unaccompanied by any activity whatever, mere presence in the city being the test. Moreover, circumstances which might move one to inquire as to the necessity of registration are completely lacking.' Like out sister circuits we find this last statement – regarding 'circumstances which might move one to inquire as to the necessity of registration' – to be critical."), citing, *United States v. Whaley*, 577 F.3d 254, 262 (5th Cir. 2009); *United States v. Gould*, 568 F.3d 459, 468-69 (4th Cir. 2009); *United States v. Dixon*, 551 F.3d 578, 584 (7h Cir. 2009); *United States v. Hinckley*, 550 F.3d 926, 938 (10th Cir. 2009); *United States v. May*, 535 F.3d 912, 921 (8th Cir. 2008); see also, *United States v. Gagnon*, 621 F.3d 30, 33 (1st Cir. 2010); *United States v. W.B.H.*, 664 F.3d 848, 852-60 (11th Cir. 2011); *United States v. Elkins*, 683 F.3d 1039, 1049-50 (9th Cir. 2012).

[79] *United States v. Pendleton*, 636 F.3d 78, 86 (3d Cir. 2011)("Pendleton's federal duty to register under SORNA was not dependent upon his duty to register under Delaware law. A person of ordinary intelligence would not assume that as long as he or she complied with state law on a particular issue, there would be no risk of running afoul of federal law"). The Sixth Circuit expressed a possible due process concern that it was not required to address but one that might arise "where an inconsistency between federal and non-complying state regimes would render it impractical, or even impossible, for an offender to register under federal law," *United States v. Felts*, 674 F.3d 599, 605 (6th Cir. 2012). The affirmative defense in §2250(b), discussed earlier, seems to designed to address this concern.

[80] *Washington v. Glucksberg*, 521 U.S. 702, 727 (1997)

[81] See, *United States v. Ambert*, 561 F.3d 1202, 1208-209 (11th Cir. 2009)(rejecting a substantive due process claim)

[82] *Saenz v. Roe*, 526 U.S. 489, 500 (1999).

[83] *United States v. Shenandoah*, 595 F.3d 151, 162-62 (3d Cir. 2010); *United States v. Ambert*, 561 F.3d 1202, 1209-210 (11th Cir. 2009); cf., *Bacon v. Neer*, 631 F.3d 875, 878 (8th Cir. 2011).

[84] U.S. Const. Amend. VIII.

[85] *Graham v. Florida*, 130 S.Ct. 2011, 2021 (2010).

[86] *United States v. Martin*, 677 F.3d 818, 822 (8th Cir. 2012).

[87] *United States v. Under Seal*, 709 F.3d 257, 263-66 (4th Cir. 2013)(not punishment); *United States v. Martin,* 677 F.3d 818, 821-22 (8th Cir. 2012)(10-year sentence "was not grossly disproportionate to [the] offense"); *United States v. Juvenile Male*, 670 F.3d 999, 1010 (9th Cir 2012)("Given the high standard that is required to establish cruel and unusual punishment, we hold that SORNA's registration requirements do not violate the Eighth Amendment"); *United States v. May*, 535 F.3d 912, 920 (8th Cir. 2008)(not punishment).

[88] U.S. Const. Amend. X ("The powers not delegated to the United States by the Constitution, nor prohibited by it to the States, are reserved to the States respectively, or to the people").

[89] U.S. Const. Art. I, §8, cls. 1, 3, 18 ("The Congress shall have Power To lay and collect Taxes, Duties, Imposts and Excises, to pay the Debts and provide for the common Defence and general Welfare of the United States ... To regulate Commerce with foreign Nations, and among the several States, and with the Indian Tribes; ... And To make all Laws which shall be necessary and proper for carrying into Execution the foregoing Powers, and all other Powers vested by this Constitution in the Government of the United States, or in any Department or Officer thereof").

[90] Cf., U.S. Const. Art. I, §8, cl. 18.

[91] *United States v. Johnson*, 632 F.3d 912, 919 (5th Cir. 2011)("The First, Second, Third, Eighth, and Tenth Circuits have held that private parties do not having standing to bring such claims. the Seventh and Eleventh Circuits have permitted private parties to assert Tenth Amendment claims").

[92] *United States v. Shenandoah*, 595 F.3d 151, 161-62 (3d Cir. 2010)("Shenandoah argues that SORNA is unconstitutional because it compels New York law enforcement to accept registrations from federally-mandated sex offender programs in violation of the Tenth Amendment.... We need not tarry long on this argument, because Shenandoah lacks standing to raise this issue"); *United States v. Zuniga*, 579 F.3d 845, 851 (8th Cir. 2009).

[93] *Bond v. United States*, 131 S.Ct. 2355, 2363-364 (2011); see also, *United States v. Felts*, 674 F.3d 599, 607 (6th Cir. 2012)("The United States counters that Felts lacks standing to assert SORNA's alleged violation. This is no longer an accurate statement of law. The United States' brief was filed on June 6, 2011, ten days before the Supreme Court decided *Bond*.... An individual can assert that the enforcement of a law violates the Tenth Amendment, particularly when a defendant has a significant liberty interest at stake. Because Felts was prosecuted for violating SORNA, he has standing to challenge the act for being enforced in violation of the Tenth Amendment").

[94] *Reynolds v. United States*, 132 S.Ct. 975, 984 (2012); see also, *United States v. Knutson*, 680 F.3d 1021, 1023 (8th Cir. 2012)("This court had previously held that pre-Act offenders lack standing to challenge SORNA. However, after the parties filed their briefs, the Supreme Court ruled that pre-Act offenders have standing to challenge SORNA under the non-delegation doctrine. *Reynolds*, 132 S.Ct. at 984").

[95] U.S. Const. Art. I, §8, cl. 1.

[96] *South Dakota v. Dole*, 483 U.S. 203, 207 (1987).

[97] *Id.* at 207-208.

[98] *National Federation of Independent Business v. Sebelius*, 132 S.Ct. 2566, 2601-607 (Roberts, Ch.J. joined by Breyer and Kagan, JJ.); 132 S.Ct. at 2656-667 (Scalia, J. with Kennedy, Thomas, and Alito, JJ.)(dissenting).

[99] Cf., *Id.* at 2604-605 (Roberts, Ch.J.)("It is ease to see how the *Dole* Court could conclude that the threatened loss of less than half of one percent of South Dakota's budget left that State with a 'prerogative' to reject Congress's desired policy, 'not merely in theory but in fact.' The threatened loss of over 10 percent of a State's overall budget, in contrast, is economic dragooning that leaves the States with no real option but to acquiesce in the Medicaid expansion"); *id.* at 2659 (Scalia, J.)(dissenting)("[W]hile Congress may seek to induce States to accept conditional grants, Congress may not cross the 'point at which pressure turns into compulsion, and ceases to be inducement"). See generally CRS Report R42367, *Medicaid and Federal Grant Conditions After* NFIB v. Sebelius*: Constitutional Issues and Analysis*.

[100] 42 U.S.C. 16925(a).

[101] *New York v. United States*, 505 U.S. 144, 175-76 (1992); *Printz v. United States*, 521 U.S. 898, 935 (1997)("We held in *New York* that Congress cannot compel the States to enact or enforce a federal regulatory program. Today we hold that Congress cannot circumvent that prohibition by conscripting the States' officers directly").

[102] *United States v. Felts*, 674 F.3d 599, 608 (2012)("SORNA does not fall under the rubric of Printz, but rather relies on Congress spending power. Failure to implement SORNA results

in a loss of 10% of federal funding under [the law enforcement assistance program]. Conditioning of funds in this manner is appropriate under *South Dakota v. Dole* (stating that Congress's power to condition the receipt of federal funds under the spending power is valid so long as (1) the spending/withholding is in the pursuit of the general welfare; (2) the conditional nature is clear and unambiguous; (3) the condition is rationally related to the purpose of the federal interest, program, or funding; and (4) the conduct required to comply with the condition is not barred by the constitution itself)"); see also, *United States v. Smith*, 655 F.3d 839, 848 (8th Cir. 2011); *United States v. Johnson*, 632 F.3d 912, 920 (5th Cir. 2011); *Kennedy v. Allera,* 612 F.3d 261, 268-70 (4th Cir. 2010); *United States v. Guzman*, 591 F.3d 83, 95 (2d Cir. 2010).

[103] The Justice Department indicates that fifteen states are now in substantial compliance with SORNA requirements, *Jurisdictions That Have Substantially Implemented SORNA*, available at http://www.ojp.usdoj.gov/smart/ newsroom_jurisdictions_sorna.htm.

[104] U.S. Const. Art. I, §8, cl. 3.

[105] *United States v. Morrison*, 529 U.S. 598, 608-609 (2000), citing inter alia, *United States v. Lopez*, 514 U.S. 549, 558-59 (1995). Of late, seven Members of the Court have explained that the Commerce Clause does not authorize Congress to punish those who elect not to engage in commerce, *National Federation of Independent Business v. Sebelius*, 132 S.Ct. 2566, 2591 (Roberts, Ch.J. joined by Breyer and Kagan, JJ.)("The individual mandate forces individuals into commerce precisely because they elected to refrain from commercial activity. Such a law cannot be sustained under a clause authorizing Congress to 'regulate Commerce'"); 132 S.Ct. at 2644 (Scalia, J. with Kennedy, Thomas, and Alito, JJ.)(dissenting)("But that failure—that abstention from commerce—is not 'Commerce.' To be sure, purchasing insurance is 'Commerce'; but one does not regulate commerce that does not exist by compelling its existence").

[106] *United States v. Coleman*, 675 F.3d 615, 620 (6th Cir. 2012), citing in accord, *United States v. George*, 625 F.3d 1124, 1129-130 (9th Cir. 2010); *United States v. Parks*. 698 F.3d 1, 6-7 (1st Cir. 2012); *United States v. Vasquez*, 611 F.3d 325, 330-31 (7th Cir. 2010); *United States v. Shenandoah*, 595 F.3d 151, 160 (3d Cir. 2010); *United States v. Guzman*, 591 F.3d 83, 89-92 (2d Cir. 2010); *United States v. Whaley*, 577 F.3d 254, 259-61 (5th Cir. 2009); *United States v. Gould*, 568 F.3d 459, 470-75 (4th Cir. 2009); *United States v. Ambert*, 561 F.3d 1202, 1210-212 (11th Cir. 2009); *United States v. Lawrence*, 548 F.3d 1329, 1337 (10th Cir. 2008); and *United States v. May*, 535 F.3d 912, 911-22 (8trh Cir. 2008).

[107] *United States v. Pendleton*, 636 F.3d 78, 87-8 (3d Cir. 2011), quoting, *United States v. Guzman*, 591 F.3d 83, 90-1 (2d Cir. 2010), and citing in accord, *United States v. Vasquez*, 611 F.3d 325, 330(7th Cir. 2010); *United States v. Whaley*, 577 F.3d 254, 261 (5th Cir. 2009); *United States v. Ambert*, 561 F.3d 1202, 1211-212 (11th Cir. 2009); and *United States v. Howell*, 552 F.3d 709, 717 (8th Cir. 2009).

[108] 18 U.S.C. 4248.

[109] *United States v. Comstock*, 130 S.Ct. 1949, 1955-956 (2010).

[110] *Id*. at 1956-957, citing inter alia, *McCulloch v. Maryland*, 4 Wheat. (17 U.S.) 316, 421 (1810), and *Gonzalez v. Raich*, 545 U.S. 1, 22 (2005).

[111] *Id*. at 1963 ("[W]e must reject respondents' argument that the Necessary and Proper Clause permits no more than a single step between an enumerated power and an Act of Congress").

[112] *Id*. at 1965.

[113] *Id*. ("We take these five considerations together. They include (1) the breadth of the Necessary and Proper Clause, (2) the long history of federal involvement in this arena, (3) the sound reasons for the statute's enactment in light of the Government's custodial interest in safeguarding the public from dangers posed by those in federal custody, (4) the statute's accommodation of state interests, and (5) the statute's narrow scope. Taken together, these considerations lead us to conclude that the statute is a "necessary and proper" means of exercising the federal authority that permits Congress to create federal criminal laws.... ").

[114] *United States v. Kebodeaux*, 687 F.3d 232, 253-54 (5th Cir. 2012)(Congress lacks the legislative authority to require under SORNA "a former federal sex offender to register an intrastate change of address after he has served his sentence and has already been unconditionally released from prison and the military"), rev'd, 133 S.Ct. 2496 (2013).

[115] *United States v. Kebodeaux*, 647 F.3d 137, 138-39 (5th Cir. 2011), vac'd for reh'g en banc, 647 F.3d 605 (5th Cir. 2011).

[116] U.S. Const. Art. I, §8, cl. 14 ("The Congress shall have Power ... To make Rules for the Government and Regulation of the land and naval Forces"). Some of the analysis that follows was borrowed from a *Kebodeaux* legal sidebar, CRS, *SORNA Clears Constitutional Hurdle*.

[117] U.S. Const. Art. I, §8, cl. 18 ("The Congress shall have Power ... To make all Laws which shall be necessary and proper for carrying into Execution the foregoing powers, and all other Powers vested by this Constitution in the Government of the United States, or in any Department or Officer thereof"").

[118] *United States v. Kebodeaux*, 687 F.3d 232, 244-45 (5th Cir. 2012)("In summary, even taking into account 'the breadth of the Necessary and Proper Clause,' *Comstock,* 130 S.Ct. at 1965, SORNA's registration requirements and criminal penalty for failure to register as a sex offender, as applied to those, like Kebodeaux, who had already been unconditionally released from federal custody or supervision at the time Congress sought to regulate them, are not 'rationally related' or 'reasonably adapted' to Congress's power to criminalize federal sex offenses to begin with. The statute's regulation of an individual, after he has served his sentence and is no longer subject to federal custody or supervision, solely because he once committed a federal crime, (1) is novel and unprecedented despite over 200 years of federal criminal law, (2) is not "reasonably adapted" to the government's custodial interest in its prisoners or its interest in punishing federal criminals, (3) is unprotective of states' sovereign interest over what intrastate conduct to criminalize within their own borders, and (4) is sweeping in the scope of its reasoning").

[119] *United States v. Kebodeaux*, 133 S.Ct. at 2501 ("[W]e need not go much further than the Circuit's critical assumption that Kebdeaux's release was 'unconditional,' i.e., that after Kebodeaux's release, he was not in 'any ... special relationship with the federal government.' To the contrary, the Solicitor General, tracing through a complex set of statutory cross-references, has pointed out that at the time of his offense and conviction Kebodeaux was subject to the federal Wetterling Act, an Act that imposed upon him registration requirements very similar to those that SORNA later mandated").

[120] 42 U.S.C. 14072(i)(1994 ed., Supp. IV).

[121] *United States v. Kebodeaux*, 133 S.Ct. at 2502 ("No one here claims that the Wetterling Act, as applied to military sex offenders like Kebodeaux, falls outside the scope of the Necessary and Proper Clause. And it is difficult to see how anyone could persuasively do so").

[122] *Id.* at 2505 ("SORNA's more specific changes reflect Congress' determination that the statute, changed in respect to frequency, penalties and other details, will keep track of more officers and will encourage States themselves to adopt its uniform standards. No one here claims that these changes are unreasonable or that Congress could not reasonably have found them 'necessary and proper' means for furthering its pre-existing registration ends").

[123] U.S. Const. Art. I, §1.

[124] *Panama Refining Co. v. Ryan*, 293 U.S. 388, 421 (1935); see also, *Schechter Corp. v. United States*, 295 U.S. 495, 529 (1935).

[125] *Hampton & Co. v. United States*, 276 U.S. 294, 409 (1928)("If Congress shall lay down by legislative act an intelligible principle to which the person or body authorized to [perform the delegated task] is directed to conform, such legislative action is not a forbidden delegation of legislative power"); see also, *American Power Co. v. S.E.C.*, 329 U.S. 90, 105 (1946)("The legislative process would frequently bog down if Congress were constitutionally required to appraise before-hand the myriad situations to which it wishes a particular policy to be applied and to formulate specific rules for each situation. Necessity

therefore fixes a point beyond which it is unreasonable and impracticable to compel Congress to prescribe detailed rules; it then becomes constitutionally sufficient if Congress clearly delineates the general policy, the public agency which is to apply it, and the boundaries of this delegated authority"); *Whitman v. American Trucking Ass'ns, Inc.*, 531 U.S. 457, 474-75 (2001)("The scope of discretion §109(b)(1) allows is in fact well within the outer limits of our nondelegation precedents. In the history of the Court we have found the requisite "intelligible principle" lacking in only two statutes, one of which provided literally no guidance for the exercise of discretion, and the other of which conferred authority to regulate the entire economy on the basis of no more precise a standard than stimulating the economy by assuring 'fair competition.' ... [W]e have 'almost never felt qualified to second-guess Congress regarding the permissible degree of policy judgment that can be left to those executing or applying the law'").

[126] *United States v. Fernandez*, 710 F.3d 847, 849-50 (8th Cir. 2013)("SORNA's broad policy statement that it was designed 'to protect the public from sex offenders and offenders against children' [is] 'sufficient to provide an intelligible principle for delegation'"); *United States v. Parks*, 698 F.3d 1, 7-8 (1st Cir. 2012); *United States v.Felts*, 674 F.3d 599, 606 (6th Cir. 2012); *United States v. Guzman*, 591 F.3d 83, 92-3 (2d Cir. 2010); *United States v. Whaley*, 577 F.3d 254, 263-64(5th Cir. 2009); *United States v. Ambert*, 561 F.3d 1202, 1212-214 (11th Cir. 2009).

INDEX

M

N

O

P

Q

R

S

T

U

V

W

Y